The Best Low Fat High Protein Cookbook

Delicious High-Protein Recipes for a Healthier You

BY ELLA ROSEMARY

Copyright © by Ella Rosemary

No part of this publication may be reproduced, distributed, or transmitted in any form or by any means, including photocopying, recording, or other electronic or mechanical methods, without the prior written permission of the publisher, except in the case of brief quotations embodied in critical reviews and specific other noncommercial uses permitted by copyright law.

This book is a work of authorship by Ella Rosemary. It has been published with the intention to provide high-quality, low-fat, high-protein recipes to those seeking a healthier lifestyle. The content within "The Best Low Fat High Protein Cookbook: Delicious High-Protein Recipes for a Healthier You" is the result of the author's original work and has not been copied from any other source.

The recipes and content presented in this book are for personal use only and may not be sold or used for commercial purposes without express permission from the author. The information in this cookbook is intended to be educational and not for the diagnosis, prescription, or treatment of any health disorder. This information should be different from consultation with a competent healthcare professional.

The views expressed by the author are solely her own and do not necessarily reflect the publisher's opinions. The publisher and author present this book without any warranties and do not guarantee any results from using the recipes contained herein. They will not be liable for any damages arising from using this book, including but not limited to direct, indirect, incidental, punitive, and consequential damages.

Table of Contents

Introduction

Are you looking to transform your diet and improve your health without sacrificing taste and enjoyment? Look no further!
"The Best Low Fat High Protein Cookbook: Delicious High-Protein Recipes for a Healthier You" by **Ella Rosemary** is the ultimate guide for anyone seeking to boost their protein intake while keeping fats to a minimum. This cookbook is filled with mouth-watering recipes that are nutritious and incredibly delicious.

Imagine indulging in dishes that not only tantalize your taste buds but also contribute to your well-being. With Ella Rosemary's expertly crafted recipes, you can enjoy various meals that will satisfy and energize you. From hearty breakfasts to sumptuous dinners, each recipe is designed to be easy to follow and perfect for any occasion.

Take the first step towards a healthier you by embracing the high-protein, low-fat lifestyle. Whether you want to lose weight, build muscle, or maintain a balanced diet, this cookbook has everything you need to achieve your goals. So, read **"The Best Low Fat High Protein Cookbook"** today and start enjoying the benefits of a healthier, happier life!

Chapter 01

What is a low-fat high-protein diet?

A low-fat, high-protein diet is an eating plan that emphasizes foods rich in protein but low in fat, such as fish, skinless poultry, lean meat, legumes, eggs, and low-fat dairy products. This diet promotes weight loss, muscle mass, bone health, and appetite control.

Some examples of low-fat, high-protein foods are:

➢ Plain or Greek yogurt
➢ Egg whites
➢ Skimmed or dry milk
➢ Tofu
➢ Lentils
➢ Beans
➢ Quinoa
➢ Turkey breast
➢ Chicken breast
➢ Salmon
➢ Tuna
➢ Cod

A typical day on a low-fat, high-protein diet may look something like this: **Breakfast**: Greek yogurt with fresh berries and granola. **Snack**: Hard-boiled egg whites and an apple. **Lunch**: Turkey and cheese sandwich on whole-wheat bread with lettuce, tomato, and mustard. **Snack**: Low-fat cottage cheese with pineapple chunks. **Dinner**: Grilled salmon with roasted broccoli and brown rice. **Dessert**: Skimmed milk with a small piece of dark chocolate

A low-fat, high-protein diet can be a healthy and satisfying way to eat as long as you balance your protein intake with other nutrients, such as carbs, fiber, vitamins, minerals, and healthy fats. You should also drink plenty of water and limit your intake of processed foods, added sugars, and alcohol

This helps you understand a low-fat, high-protein diet and how to follow it.

How much protein should be eaten per day?

The amount of protein you need daily depends on many factors, such as weight, age, activity level, and health goals. According to the Food and Drug Administration, the recommended daily protein intake for most US adults is around 50 grams (g), but this may vary depending on your needs.

Some general guidelines for protein intake are:

- ✓ Aim for around 30% of your calories from protein, or about 0.8-1.2 g per pound of body weight, for weight loss.
- ✓ Aim for around 30% of your calories from protein, or about 1-1.5 g per pound of body weight for muscle gain.
- ✓ For weight maintenance, aim for around 15-25% of your calories from protein, or about 0.5-0.8 g per pound of body weight.
- ✓ Aim for around 25% of your calories from protein, or about 0.8-1 g per pound of pre-pregnancy weight for pregnancy.

Protein is found in many foods, such as meat, eggs, dairy, beans, nuts, seeds and soy. You can also use protein supplements, such as powders, bars, or shakes, to boost your intake. However, choosing high-quality protein sources that provide all the essential amino acids and other nutrients is important.

Protein is essential for your health, as it helps build and repair tissues, make enzymes and hormones, and support your immune system. Eating enough protein can also help you feel full, increase your metabolism, and preserve muscle mass.

You can use this to calculate your specific protein needs based on your weight, goal, and activity level. Adjust your protein intake as your body changes and your goals evolve.

Which foods that are high in protein have what risks??

A high protein diet may have some benefits, such as increasing satiety and retaining muscle, but it may also have some risks, such as:

- Weight gain occurs if you consume too many calories and excess protein is stored as fat.
- Lousy breath, headache, and constipation if you limit your carbohydrate and fiber intake.
- Heart disease and colon cancer if you overeat red meat and processed meat that are high in saturated fat.
- Kidney problems include kidney disease or consuming more protein than your body can handle.

These risks may vary depending on the type, quality, and quantity of protein you eat and your overall health and lifestyle. Therefore, you should consult your healthcare provider before starting a high-protein diet and choose your protein sources carefully. It would help to balance your protein intake with enough carbohydrates, fiber, fruits, and vegetables to meet your nutritional needs.

Which food is high in protein?

Many foods are high in protein, an essential nutrient for your health. Some examples of high-protein foods are:

- Eggs: One large egg (50 g) provides 6.3 g of protein.
- Almonds: One ounce (28.35 g) provides 6 g of protein.
- Chicken breast: One-half of a chicken breast (86 g) provides 26.7 g of protein.
- Cottage cheese: One cup (226 g) of cottage cheese provides 28 g of protein.
- Salmon: One salmon fillet (178 g) contains 39.3 g protein.

You can also find high-protein foods in other categories, such as lean meats, fish, dairy, soy, legumes, seeds, nuts, and grains. Eating protein-rich foods can help you feel full and satisfied and support your muscle mass and overall health.

How to control your weight by eating low fat and high protein diet?

To control your weight by eating a low-fat, high-protein diet, you can follow these general steps:

- ✓ Calculate your daily calorie needs based on age, gender, activity level, and weight goals.
- ✓ Aim to get at least 20% of your calories from protein, and limit your fat intake to less than 30% of your calories.
- ✓ Choose low-fat, high-protein foods like lean meats, eggs, dairy, soy, legumes, nuts, seeds, and protein powders.
- ✓ Include some complex carbohydrates, such as whole grains, fruits, and vegetables, to provide fiber and other nutrients.
- ✓ Avoid foods high in added sugars, sodium, saturated fats, trans fats, and cholesterol.
- ✓ Drink plenty of water and limit your intake of sugary drinks, alcohol, and caffeine.
- ✓ Eat smaller portions and spread your meals throughout the day to keep your metabolism and appetite in check.
- ✓ Combine your diet with regular physical activity, such as aerobic, strength, and flexibility exercises.

Following a low-fat, high-protein diet can help you lose weight and improve your health by reducing your appetite, boosting your metabolism, preserving your muscle mass, and supporting your bone health. However, you should consult your doctor before starting any new diet plan, especially if you have any medical conditions or allergies.

What types of foods should be avoided?

According to some sources, some of the foods that you should avoid or limit are:

- ➢ French fries and potato chips: These are high in calories, fat, and acrylamides, which are linked to cancer.

- ➢ Sugary drinks: These are high in calories and added sugar, which can lead to weight gain and other health problems.
- ➢ White bread: This is highly refined and often contains added sugar. It also lacks protein and fiber and can spike your blood sugar levels.
- ➢ Candy bars are high in sugar, refined carbs, and unhealthy fats. They also have little nutritional value and can cause cravings.
- ➢ Some fruit juices: These are often loaded with sugar and lack the fiber and phytochemicals of whole fruits. They can also increase your calorie intake and blood sugar levels.
- ➢ Pastries, cookies, and cakes are high in sugar, refined flour, and unhealthy fats. They also contain artificial ingredients and preservatives, which can harm your health.
- ➢ Some types of alcohol (especially beer): These are high in calories and can interfere with your metabolism and liver function. They can also lower your inhibitions and make you eat more.
- ➢ Ice cream is high in calories, sugar, and saturated fat. It can also trigger cravings and overeating, especially if you eat it as a comfort food.
- ➢ Pizza is high in calories, refined carbs, and saturated fat. It can also contain processed meats, cheese, and sauces high in sodium and additives.
- ➢ High-calorie coffee drinks: These are often loaded with sugar, cream, and syrups, which can add hundreds of calories to your diet. They can also affect your blood sugar and insulin levels.
- ➢ Foods high in added sugar or salt: These include processed foods, fast foods, snacks, sauces, dressings, and condiments. They can increase your calorie intake, blood pressure, and risk of chronic diseases.

You should avoid or limit these foods if you want to lose weight or improve your health. However, you don't have to cut them out completely. You can still enjoy them occasionally in moderation, as part of a balanced and varied diet.

Chapter 02: Healthy And Hearty Breakfasts

Recipe 01: Healthy Breakfast Egg With Avocado and Toast

Start your day with this delicious and nutritious breakfast that combines whole wheat toast, creamy avocado, and perfectly poached eggs. This recipe is easy to make and ready in under 15 minutes. It's also low in fat and protein, making it an excellent choice for a balanced diet. Enjoy this satisfying meal that will keep you energized for hours!

Servings: 4
Prepping Time: 5 minutes
Cook Time: 10 minutes
Difficulty: Easy
Total Time: 15 minutes

Ingredients:

- ✓ 4 slices of whole wheat bread
- ✓ 2 ripe avocados
- ✓ Juice of 1 lime
- ✓ Salt and pepper, to taste
- ✓ 4 eggs
- ✓ 2 teaspoons of white vinegar
- ✓ Optional: red pepper flakes, cilantro, olive oil, flaky sea salt

Step-by-Step Preparation:

1. Toast the bread in a toaster or oven until golden and crisp.
2. Cut the avocados in half, remove the pits, and scoop the flesh into a small bowl. Mash with a fork and add the lime juice, salt, and pepper. Mix well and set aside.
3. Fill a large saucepan with water and bring to a boil. Reduce the heat to a simmer and add the vinegar. Crack one egg into a small bowl and gently slide it into the water. Repeat with the remaining eggs, leaving some space between them. Poach for about 3 minutes or until the whites are set and the yolks are still runny. Use a slotted spoon to transfer the eggs to a plate lined with paper towels.
4. Spread the avocado mixture evenly over the toast slices. Top each with a poached egg and sprinkle with some red pepper flakes, cilantro, olive oil, and flaky sea salt, if desired. Serve hot or at room temperature.

Nutritional Facts: (Per serving)

- Calories: 367
- Fat: 23 g
- Carbohydrates: 32 g
- Fiber: 11 g
- Protein: 14 g
- Sodium: 216 mg
- Potassium: 781 mg
- Vitamin C: 15 mg
- Calcium: 86 mg
- Iron: 3 mg

The web search results from Inspire this recipe and. You can check them out for more tips and variations. I hope you enjoy this healthy breakfast, whole wheat toasted bread with avocado and poached egg recipe. Let me know how it turns out!

Recipe 02: Sweet Chickpeas Pancakes Broccoli With Carrots

If you're looking for a low-fat, high-protein breakfast packed with veggies, try these savory pancakes made of chickpea flour and grated broccoli, carrots, and cauliflower. Chickpea flour is gluten-free, rich in fiber, and easy to use. It creates a nutty, custardy batter that cooks into fluffy pancakes. You can top them with your favorite sauce, cheese, or herbs for a satisfying and delicious meal.

Servings: 4
Prepping Time: 15 minutes
Cook Time: 15 minutes
Difficulty: Easy
Total Time: 30 minutes

Ingredients:
- ✓ 1 cup chickpea flour
- ✓ 1 teaspoon baking powder
- ✓ 1/2 teaspoon salt
- ✓ 1/4 teaspoon black pepper
- ✓ 1 cup water

- ✓ 2 tablespoons oil, divided
- ✓ 1 cup grated broccoli
- ✓ 1 cup grated carrots
- ✓ 1 cup grated cauliflower
- ✓ Optional: yogurt, sour cream, salsa, cheese, parsley, etc.

Step-by-Step Preparation:

1. Whisk together the chickpea flour, baking powder, salt, and pepper in a large bowl. Gradually whisk in the water, and 1 tablespoon of oil until smooth and no lumps remain. Stir in the grated broccoli, carrots, and cauliflower.
2. Heat a nonstick skillet over medium-high heat and lightly grease with some oil. Drop 1/4 cup of batter onto the skillet and spread it into a thin circle. Cook for about 3 minutes or until bubbles form on the surface. Flip and cook for another 2 minutes or until golden and cooked through. Repeat with the remaining batter, adding more oil as needed.
3. Serve the pancakes hot or warm, with your choice of toppings.

Nutritional Facts: (Per serving)

- Calories: 232
- Fat: 10 g
- Carbohydrates: 28 g
- Fiber: 7 g
- Protein: 9 g
- Sodium: 372 mg
- Potassium: 543 mg
- Vitamin A: 106% DV
- Vitamin C: 64% DV
- Calcium: 9% DV
- Iron: 14% DV

The web search results from Inspire this recipe and. You can check them out for more tips and variations. I hope you enjoy these pancakes of chickpeas, broccoli, carrots, and cauliflower. Let me know how they turn out!

Recipe 03: Delicious Quesadilla With Mushrooms

Who doesn't love a cheesy, crispy quesadilla? This recipe takes it to the next level by adding sautéed mushrooms and a spicy, sour cream sauce. It's a quick and easy breakfast with low fat and protein. You can use any mushrooms, such as button, cremini, or wild. Serve these quesadillas with some lime wedges, pickled onions, and cilantro for a burst of freshness.

Servings: 4
Prepping Time: 10 minutes
Cook Time: 15 minutes
Difficulty: Easy
Total Time: 25 minutes

Ingredients:
- ✓ 8 small flour tortillas
- ✓ 2 cups shredded cheddar cheese
- ✓ 2 tablespoons butter
- ✓ 1 tablespoon oil
- ✓ 1 pound mushrooms, sliced
- ✓ Salt and pepper, to taste
- ✓ 1/2 cup sour cream
- ✓ 2 teaspoons hot sauce, or more to taste

✓ Optional: lime wedges, pickled red onions, cilantro leaves

Step-by-Step Preparation:
1. In a small bowl, whisk together the sour cream and hot sauce. Adjust the spiciness to your liking. Set aside.
2. Heat the oil and melt the butter in a large skillet over medium-high heat. Add the mushrooms and cook, stirring occasionally, for about 15 minutes or until browned and tender. Season with salt and pepper.
3. Wipe the skillet clean and place it back over medium heat. Place one tortilla on the skillet and sprinkle 1/4 cup of cheese over half of it. Spoon 1/4 of the mushroom mixture over the cheese and fold the tortilla in half. Press lightly to seal. Cook for about 2 minutes per side or until golden and crisp. Transfer to a cutting board and keep warm. Repeat with the remaining tortillas, cheese, and mushrooms.
4. Cut the quesadillas into wedges and serve with the sour cream sauce and the optional toppings.

Nutritional Facts: (Per serving)
- Calories: 543
- Fat: 34 g
- Carbohydrates: 38 g
- Fiber: 3 g
- Protein: 24 g
- Sodium: 631 mg
- Potassium: 608 mg
- Vitamin A: 18% DV
- Vitamin C: 5% DV
- Calcium: 47% DV
- Iron: 16% DV

The web search results from Inspire this recipe and. You can check them out for more tips and variations. I hope you enjoy these pieces of quesadilla with mushrooms, sour cream, and cheese. Let me know how they turn out!

Recipe 04: Healthy Oatmeal With Berries

Start your day with this satisfying and energizing breakfast packed with protein, fiber, and flavor. You will love the combination of scrambled eggs, cheese, and salsa wrapped in a warm tortilla, served with a side of crispy bacon, fresh salad, and juice. This recipe is easy to make and can be customized to your taste. Enjoy!

Servings: 4
Prepping Time: 15 minutes
Cook Time: 15 minutes
Difficulty: Easy
Total Time: 30 minutes

Ingredients:
- ✓ 8 eggs
- ✓ 1/4 cup milk
- ✓ Salt and pepper, to taste
- ✓ 1 tablespoon butter
- ✓ 1 cup shredded cheddar cheese
- ✓ 1/4 cup salsa
- ✓ 4 large flour tortillas
- ✓ 8 slices bacon

✓ 4 cups mixed salad greens
✓ 1/4 cup salad dressing of your choice
✓ 4 cups juice of your choice

Step-by-Step Preparation:

. whisk together the eggs, milk, salt, and pepper in a medium bowl. Set aside.

. In a large skillet over medium-high heat, cook the bacon until crisp, turning occasionally, for about 10 minutes. Drain on paper towels and keep warm.

. In the same skillet, melt the butter over medium-low heat. Add the egg mixture and cook, stirring occasionally, until scrambled, for about 10 minutes. Stir in the cheese and salsa and keep warm.

. In a small skillet over medium-high heat, warm the tortillas, one at a time, or about 10 seconds per side. Transfer to a plate and cover with a damp cloth to keep warm.

. To assemble the burritos, spoon about 1/4 of the egg mixture onto the center of each tortilla. Fold the bottom edge over the filling, then fold in the sides and roll up tightly.

. To serve, cut the burritos in half and place them on a large platter. Serve with the bacon, salad, and juice.

Nutritional Facts: (Per serving)
- Calories: 720
- Fat: 36 g
- Carbohydrates: 62 g
- Fiber: 4 g
- Protein: 37 g

This breakfast is a great way to start your day with a balanced meal that will keep you full and energized for hours. You can also make the burritos ahead of time and freeze them for a quick and easy breakfast on the go. Just wrap them individually in foil and reheat them in the oven or microwave when ready to eat. Enjoy!

Recipe 05: Healthy Low Carb Breakfast Scrambled Eggs

Start your day with a delicious and nutritious breakfast low in carbs and protein. This easy recipe features fluffy scrambled eggs with ricotta cheese and spinach, topped with fresh berries and nuts for a burst of flavor and crunch. It's a satisfying and balanced meal that energizes you for hours.

Servings: 4
Prepping Time: 5 minutes
Cook Time: 10 minutes
Difficulty: Easy
Total Time: 15 minutes

Ingredients:
- ✓ 8 eggs
- ✓ 1/4 cup ricotta cheese
- ✓ 2 tablespoons cream (optional)
- ✓ Salt and pepper, to taste
- ✓ 2 cups spinach, washed
- ✓ 2 tablespoons butter or coconut oil for frying

✓ 1 cup mixed berries, such as strawberries, blueberries, raspberries, or blackberries
✓ 1/4 cup chopped nuts, such as almonds, walnuts, or pistachios
✓ Cheese or nutritional yeast for topping (optional)

Step-by-Step Preparation:
1. In a medium bowl, whisk the eggs, ricotta cheese, cream (if using), and salt and pepper until well combined.
2. Melt the butter or coconut oil in a large skillet over medium-low heat. Pour the egg mixture into the skillet and cook, stirring occasionally, until the eggs are set but still moist, about 10 minutes.
3. Add the spinach and toss to wilt, about 2 minutes.
4. Divide the scrambled eggs among four plates. Top with the berries, nuts, cheese, or nutritional yeast if desired. Enjoy!

Nutritional Facts: (Per serving)
- Calories: 375
- Fat: 28 g
- Carbs: 12 g
- Fiber: 4 g
- Protein: 20 g

This recipe is based on the web search results: "Healthy low-carb breakfast plate with homemade scrambled eggs, fresh berries, and nuts."

Recipe 06: Freshly Spinach and Feta Cheese Muffins

Start your day with these freshly baked spinach and feta cheese muffins. They're a perfect low-fat, high-protein breakfast option that will satisfy you throughout the morning.

Servings: 4 people
Prepping Time: 15 minutes
Cook Time: 20 minutes
Difficulty: Easy
Total Time: 35 minutes

Ingredients:
- ✓ 2 cups of spinach
- ✓ 1 cup of feta cheese
- ✓ 2 cups of whole wheat flour
- ✓ 2 eggs
- ✓ 1 cup of milk
- ✓ 1 tsp of baking powder
- ✓ Salt and pepper to taste

Step-by-Step Preparation:
1. Preheat the oven to 180°C.
2. Mix the flour, baking powder, salt, and pepper in a bowl.
3. In another bowl, whisk the eggs and milk together.
4. Gradually add the dry ingredients to the wet ingredients.
5. Fold in the spinach and feta cheese.
6. Pour the mixture into muffin tins and bake for 20 minutes.

Nutritional Facts: (Per serving)
- Calories: 220
- Protein: 12g
- Fat: 8g
- Carbohydrates: 28g
- Fiber: 4g

Enjoy these delicious muffins as a quick breakfast or a healthy snack. They're tasty and packed with nutrients, making them a great addition to your morning routine.

Recipe 07: Delicious Salmon Wrap

Kickstart your day with these delicious and nutritious Rolls with Salmon and Greens in Pita Bread. This low-fat, high-protein breakfast dish will keep you energized throughout the morning.

Servings: 4 people
Prepping Time: 15 minutes
Cook Time: 10 minutes
Difficulty: Easy
Total Time: 25 minutes

Ingredients:
- ✓ 4 pita breads
- ✓ 200g smoked salmon
- ✓ 1 cup mixed greens (spinach, arugula, etc.)
- ✓ 1/2 cup low-fat cream cheese
- ✓ Salt and pepper to taste

Step-by-Step Preparation:
1. Spread cream cheese on each pita bread.
2. Layer smoked salmon and mixed greens on top.
3. Season with salt and pepper.

4. Roll up the pita bread and cut it into halves.

Nutritional Facts: (Per serving)
- Calories: 210
- Protein: 15g
- Fat: 5g
- Carbohydrates: 25g

Enjoy this quick and easy recipe that tastes great and contributes to a healthy diet. Perfect for those busy mornings when you need a grab-and-go meal!

Recipe 08: Raspberry and Blueberry Smoothie Bowls

Start your day with a refreshing and healthy summer acai smoothie bowl. This smoothie bowl is thick, creamy, and contains antioxidants and protein. You can customize it with your favorite toppings, such as fresh fruits, granola, coconut, honey, and nut butter. It's a delicious and satisfying way to enjoy a low-fat, high-protein breakfast or snack.

☐ **Servings:** 4
Prepping Time: 10 minutes
Cook Time: 0 minutes
Difficulty: Easy
Total Time: 10 minutes

Ingredients:
- ✓ 4 frozen acai packs
- ✓ 2 cups frozen raspberries
- ✓ 2 frozen bananas
- ✓ 1 cup frozen blueberries
- ✓ 1 cup apple juice
- ✓ 4 tablespoons almond butter

- ✓ 4 tablespoons honey
- ✓ 4 tablespoons granola
- ✓ 4 tablespoons unsweetened coconut flakes
- ✓ Fresh fruits of your choice, such as bananas, blueberries, raspberries, kiwi, and mango

Step-by-Step Preparation:

1. Break the frozen acai packs into chunks and add them to a blender with frozen raspberries, bananas, blueberries, and apple juice. Blend until smooth and thick, adding more liquid to adjust the consistency.
2. Divide the smoothie mixture among four bowls and smooth the tops with a spoon.
3. Drizzle each bowl with one tablespoon of almond butter and honey.
4. Sprinkle each bowl with one tablespoon of granola and one tablespoon of coconut flakes.
5. Top each bowl with fresh fruits of your choice, such as sliced bananas, blueberries, raspberries, kiwi, and mango.
6. Enjoy your summer acai smoothie bowl with a spoon.

Nutritional Facts: (Per serving)

- Calories: 511
- Fat: 23 g
- Carbohydrates: 72 g
- Fiber: 14 g
- Protein: 10 g
- Sugar: 46 g

This summer acai smoothie bowl recipe is a great way to enjoy the seasonal fruits and boost your energy levels. It's easy to make, vegan-friendly, and gluten-free. You can also make it ahead of time and freeze it for later. Just thaw it slightly and add your toppings before serving. Try this recipe today, and let me know what you think. I hope you love it as much as I do.

Recipe 09: Healthy Vegan Sandwiches With Chickpeas

Try these vegan open sandwiches with guacamole, tofu, and chickpeas if you want a simple, satisfying, and nutritious breakfast or snack. They are packed with protein, fiber, healthy fats, and flavor. You can make them in minutes with just a few ingredients and enjoy them on your favorite bread. They are also low in fat and gluten-free.

Servings: 4
Prepping Time: 15 minutes
Cook Time: 10 minutes
Difficulty: Easy
Total Time: 25 minutes

Ingredients:
- ✓ 8 slices of whole wheat bread or gluten-free bread
- ✓ 1 ripe avocado
- ✓ 2 tablespoons of lemon juice
- ✓ Salt and pepper, to taste
- ✓ 1 block of firm tofu, drained and pressed
- ✓ 2 teaspoons of oil

- ✓ 2 teaspoons of soy sauce or tamari
- ✓ 1 teaspoon of smoked paprika
- ✓ 1/4 teaspoon of garlic powder
- ✓ 1 cup of cooked chickpeas or canned chickpeas, rinsed and drained
- ✓ 2 tablespoons of vegan mayonnaise
- ✓ 2 tablespoons of chopped parsley
- ✓ 4 lettuce leaves
- ✓ 4 tomato slices

Step-by-Step Preparation:

1. Toast the bread slices lightly in a toaster or oven.
2. Cut the avocado in half, remove the pit, and scoop out the flesh. Mash it with a fork in a small bowl and add the lemon juice, salt, and pepper. Mix well and set aside.
3. Cut the tofu into thin slices and pat them dry with paper towels. Heat the oil in a large skillet over medium-high heat and add the tofu slices. Cook for about 5 minutes, flipping once, until golden and crisp on both sides. Sprinkle with soy sauce, smoked paprika, garlic powder and toss to coat. Transfer to a plate and keep warm.
4. Mash the chickpeas with a fork in a small bowl and add the vegan mayonnaise, parsley, salt, and pepper. Mix well and set aside.
5. To assemble the sandwiches, spread the guacamole evenly over four bread slices. Top each with a lettuce leaf, tomato, and two tofu slices. Spoon the chickpea mixture over the tofu and cover with another bread slice. Cut in half and serve. Enjoy your vegan open sandwiches with guacamole, tofu, and chickpeas.

Nutritional Facts: (Per serving)

- Calories: 433
- Fat: 19 g
- Carbohydrates: 49 g
- Fiber: 13 g
- Protein: 20 g
- Sugar: 9 g

This vegan open sandwich recipe is a great way to start your day with a balanced and delicious meal. Try this recipe today, and let me know what you think. I hope you love it as much as I do.

Recipe 10: Delicious Chicken Turkey Meatballs

If you want a low-fat, high-protein breakfast or morning dish, try these homemade chicken or turkey meatballs with rice, vegetables, and tomato sauce. They are tender, juicy, flavorful, and easy to make with simple ingredients. You can serve them over fluffy rice with a rich and tangy tomato sauce and a side of steamed or roasted vegetables. They are also great for meal prep and leftovers.

Servings: 4
Prepping Time: 20 minutes
Cook Time: 40 minutes
Difficulty: Medium
Total Time: 60 minutes

Ingredients:
- ✓ 1 pound of ground chicken or turkey
- ✓ 1/4 cup of breadcrumbs
- ✓ 1/4 cup of grated parmesan cheese
- ✓ 1 egg
- ✓ 2 teaspoons of dried oregano

- ✓ Salt and pepper, to taste
- ✓ 2 tablespoons of oil
- ✓ 1 onion, chopped
- ✓ 2 garlic cloves, minced
- ✓ 1 (28-ounce) can of crushed tomatoes
- ✓ 2 teaspoons of sugar
- ✓ 1/4 cup of chopped fresh basil
- ✓ 4 cups of cooked rice
- ✓ 4 cups of mixed vegetables, such as broccoli, carrots, zucchini, or green beans

Step-by-Step Preparation:

1. Combine the ground chicken or turkey, breadcrumbs, parmesan cheese, egg, oregano, salt, and pepper in a large bowl. Mix well and shape into 16 meatballs, about the size of a golf ball.
2. Heat the oil in a large skillet over medium-high heat. Add the meatballs and cook for about 15 minutes, turning occasionally, until browned and cooked. Transfer to a plate and keep warm.
3. Add the onion and garlic in the same skillet and cook for about 10 minutes, stirring occasionally, until soft and golden. Add the crushed tomatoes, sugar, salt, and pepper and boil. Reduce the heat and simmer for about 15 minutes, until slightly thickened. Stir in the basil and taste for seasoning.
4. Return the meatballs to the sauce and simmer for another 10 minutes until heated and coated with the sauce.
5. Cook the rice according to the package directions, fluff it with a fork, and divide it among four plates. Top with the meatballs and sauce, and serve with the vegetables you choose, steamed or roasted.

Nutritional Facts: (Per serving)

- Calories: 569
- Fat: 19 g
- Carbohydrates: 67 g
- Fiber: 9 g
- Protein: 37 g
- Sugar: 15 g

This chicken or turkey meatball recipe is a hearty and satisfying meal perfect for any time of the day. Try this recipe today, and let me know what you think. I hope you love it as much as I do.

Chapter 03: Lunch with Lean and Luscious Dishes

Recipe 11: Fresh Vegetable Caesar Salad

If you love Caesar salad, you'll love this fresh vegetable version that add crunch and color to the classic dish. This salad is low in fat and protein and perfect for a lean lunch or a light dinner. It's easy to make and serves fou people.

Servings: 4
Prepping Time: 15 minutes
Cook Time: 10 minutes
Difficulty: Easy
Total Time: 25 minutes

Ingredients:
- ✓ 4 cups of chopped romaine lettuce

- ✓ 2 cups of cherry tomatoes, halved
- ✓ 1 cup of sliced cucumber
- ✓ 1/4 cup of grated Parmesan cheese
- ✓ 4 hard-boiled eggs, peeled and quartered
- ✓ 8 ounces of grilled chicken breast, sliced
- ✓ 1/4 cup of low-fat Caesar dressing
- ✓ Salt and pepper to taste
- ✓ Croutons (optional)

Step-by-Step Preparation:
1. toss the lettuce, tomatoes, cucumber, and cheese in a large salad bowl.
2. Arrange the eggs and chicken on top of the salad.
3. Drizzle the dressing over the salad and toss gently to coat.
4. Season with salt and pepper as desired.
5. Sprinkle some croutons over the salad if you like extra crunch.
6. Enjoy your fresh vegetable Caesar salad!

Nutritional Facts: (Per serving)
- Calories: 282
- Fat: 12 g
- Carbohydrates: 13 g
- Protein: 31 g
- Fiber: 3 g
- Sodium: 414 mg
- Calcium: 132 mg
- Iron: 2 mg

This fresh vegetable Caesar salad is a delicious and nutritious way to enjoy the flavors of the classic Caesar salad. It's filling, satisfying, and easy to make. You can customize it with your favorite vegetables, cheese, or dressing. Try it today and see for yourself!

Recipe 12: Turkey Taco Lettuce Wraps

If you want a light, easy, and delicious meal, you will love these Turkey Taco Lettuce Wraps. They are made with lean ground turkey, seasoned with homemade taco spices, and wrapped in crisp lettuce leaves. You can customize them with your favorite toppings, such as cheese, avocado, salsa, and sour cream. They are gluten-free, low-carb, keto, and paleo-friendly, ready in less than 30 minutes.

Servings: 4
Prepping Time: 10 minutes
Cook Time: 15 minutes
Difficulty: Easy
Total Time: 25 minutes

Ingredients:
- ✓ 1 pound of lean ground turkey
- ✓ 2 tablespoons of taco seasoning (homemade or store-bought)
- ✓ 1/4 cup of water
- ✓ 1/4 cup of tomato sauce (no sugar added)
- ✓ Salt and pepper, to taste
- ✓ 8 large lettuce leaves (romaine, iceberg, or butter)

✓ Optional toppings: shredded cheese, diced avocado, salsa, sour cream, cilantro, etc.

Step-by-Step Preparation:
1. In a large skillet over medium-high heat, cook the turkey, breaking it up with a spatula, until browned and cooked through, about 10 minutes. Drain any excess fat or liquid.
2. Add the taco seasoning, water, and tomato sauce, and stir well to combine. Simmer until slightly thickened, about 5 minutes. Season with salt and pepper, if needed.
3. To serve, spoon some turkey mixture onto each lettuce leaf and top with your desired toppings. Enjoy!

Nutritional Facts: (Per serving, without toppings)
- Calories: 216
- Protein: 37 g
- Carbohydrates: 10 g
- Fat: 3 g
- Fiber: 3 g
- Sugar: 4 g

These Turkey Taco Lettuce Wraps are a great way to enjoy the flavors of tacos without the extra carbs and calories. They are satisfying, filling, and full of protein and fiber. You can make them ahead of time and reheat them for a quick and easy lunch. They are also fun to make and eat with your family or friends. Try them today and see why they are our favorite paleo dish!

Recipe 13: Fresh Vegetable Greek Salad With Chicken

It sounds like you are looking for a recipe for grilled chicken fillet and fresh vegetable Greek salad. This delicious and healthy dish is perfect for a low-fat, high-protein lunch. Here is a possible recipe that you can try:

Servings: 4
Prepping Time: 15 minutes
Cook Time: 15 minutes
Difficulty: Easy
Total Time: 30 minutes

Ingredients:
- ✓ 4 chicken fillets, about 150 g each
- ✓ 2 teaspoons of dried oregano
- ✓ Salt and pepper, to taste
- ✓ 4 cups of chopped romaine lettuce
- ✓ 2 cups of cherry tomatoes, halved
- ✓ 1 cucumber, diced
- ✓ 1/4 cup of sliced red onion
- ✓ 1/4 cup of pitted kalamata olives

- ✓ 1/4 cup of crumbled feta cheese
- ✓ 1/4 cup of Greek yogurt
- ✓ 2 tablespoons of lemon juice
- ✓ 1 tablespoon of olive oil
- ✓ 1 garlic clove, minced
- ✓ 1 teaspoon of dried dill

Step-by-Step Preparation:

1. Preheat a grill or a grill pan over medium-high heat. Season the chicken fillets with oregano, salt, and pepper on both sides. Grill 7 minutes per side until cooked and no longer pink in the center. Transfer to a cutting board and let rest for 5 minutes, then slice thinly.
2. Toss the lettuce, tomatoes, cucumber, onion, olives, and feta cheese in a large salad bowl.
3. Whisk the yogurt, lemon juice, olive oil, garlic, dill, salt, and pepper in a small bowl until smooth and creamy.
4. Drizzle the dressing over the salad and toss to coat. Divide the salad among four plates and top with the sliced chicken. Enjoy!

Nutritional Facts: (Per serving)

- Calories: 320
- Protein: 38 g
- Fat: 13 g
- Carbohydrates: 14 g
- Fiber: 4 g
- Sugar: 8 g
- Sodium: 380 mg

This recipe is based on the web search results for "Grilled chicken fillet and fresh vegetable Greek salad recipe." You can also check out these links for more variations and tips. I hope you like this recipe and have a great lunch!

Recipe 14: Beef and Broccoli Stir Fry

If you are looking for a low-fat, high-protein, and delicious lunch dish, you will love this beef and broccoli stir fry with rice. It is easy to make, full of flavor, and ready in less than 30 minutes. You can use any beef you like if you slice it thinly and marinate it well. The broccoli adds a nice crunch and a boost of vitamins, while the rice makes it a satisfying meal. You can adjust the sauce to your taste by adding more or less soy sauce, sugar, or cornstarch.

Servings: 4
Prepping Time: 15 minutes
Cook Time: 15 minutes
Difficulty: Easy
Total Time: 30 minutes

Ingredients:
- ✓ 1/3 cup oyster sauce
- ✓ 1/3 cup sherry
- ✓ 2 teaspoons toasted sesame oil
- ✓ 1 teaspoon soy sauce
- ✓ 1 teaspoon white sugar
- ✓ 1 teaspoon cornstarch

- ✓ 3/4 pound beef round steak, cut into 1/8-inch thick strips
- ✓ 3 tablespoons vegetable oil, plus more if needed
- ✓ 1 thin slice of fresh ginger root
- ✓ 1 clove garlic, peeled and smashed
- ✓ 1 pound broccoli, cut into florets

Step-by-Step Preparation:
1. Whisk oyster sauce, sherry, sesame oil, soy sauce, sugar, and cornstarch in a bowl; stir until sugar has dissolved.
2. Add beef strips to the bowl and toss to coat. Refrigerate for at least 15 minutes to marinate.
3. Heat a large skillet or wok over high heat. Add 2 tablespoons of oil and swirl to coat. Add ginger and garlic and stir-fry for about 10 seconds or until fragrant. Remove and discard.
4. Add broccoli to the same skillet and stir-fry for about 5 minutes or until crisp-tender. Transfer to a plate and keep warm.
5. Add more oil to the skillet if needed. Add beef, marinade, and stir-fry for about 10 minutes, or until meat is cooked through and the sauce thickens.
6. Return broccoli to the skillet and toss to combine. Serve hot cooked rice.

Nutritional Facts: (Per serving)
- Calories: 387
- Fat: 19 g
- Carbohydrates: 23 g
- Protein: 31 g
- Fiber: 4 g
- Sodium: 878 mg

This beef and broccoli stir fry with rice is a great way to enjoy a restaurant-style dish at home without spending too much time or money. It is also a healthy and balanced meal that will keep you full and energized. You can make and reheat it later or freeze it for future use. Enjoy!

Recipe 15: Healthy Chickpea and Cucumber Salad

Enjoy a refreshing and satisfying salad with protein, fiber, and flavor. This easy recipe takes only 15 minutes to prepare and serves 4 people. It's perfect for a light lunch or a side dish for a summer meal.

Servings: 4
Prepping Time: 10 minutes
Cook Time: 5 minutes
Difficulty: Easy
Total Time: 15 minutes

Ingredients:
- ✓ 1 (15 oz.) can of chickpeas, drained and rinsed
- ✓ 2 cups of cherry tomatoes, halved
- ✓ 2 cups of cucumber, diced
- ✓ 2 cups of baby spinach, chopped
- ✓ 1/4 cup of red onion, thinly sliced
- ✓ 1/4 cup of fresh parsley, chopped
- ✓ 2 tablespoons of lemon juice
- ✓ 2 tablespoons of olive oil

- ✓ 1 teaspoon of dried oregano
- ✓ Salt and pepper, to taste
- ✓ Optional: 1/4 cup of crumbled feta cheese or vegan feta cheese

Step-by-Step Preparation:
1. Toss the chickpeas, tomatoes, cucumber, spinach, onion, and parsley in a large bowl.
2. Whisk the lemon juice, olive oil, oregano, salt, and pepper in a small bowl.
3. Drizzle the dressing over the salad and toss well to coat.
4. Sprinkle the feta cheese on top if desired.
5. Serve immediately or refrigerate for up to 3 days.

Nutritional Facts: (Per serving)
- Calories: 282
- Fat: 13 g
- Carbohydrates: 33 g
- Fiber: 9 g
- Protein: 11 g
- Sodium: 316 mg
- Potassium: 664 mg
- Calcium: 97 mg
- Iron: 4 mg

This salad is a great way to enjoy the season's fresh produce and get a boost of plant-based protein. You can customize it with your favorite herbs, cheese, or olives. It's also gluten-free, dairy-free, and vegan-friendly. Try it today, and let me know what you think!

Recipe 16: Cod Fillet Baked With Garlic Butter

Treat yourself to a delicious and nutritious meal that is ready in less than 30 minutes. This recipe features tender and flaky cod fillets baked in a rich, buttery garlic sauce, accompanied by crisp and tender roasted asparagus and fresh spinach. This low-fat, high-protein, and gluten-free dish serves 4 people.

Servings: 4
Prepping Time: 10 minutes
Cook Time: 15 minutes
Difficulty: Easy
Total Time: 25 minutes

Ingredients:
- ✓ 4 (6 oz.) cod fillets, skinless and boneless
- ✓ Salt and pepper, to taste
- ✓ 4 tablespoons of butter, melted
- ✓ 4 cloves of garlic, minced
- ✓ 2 teaspoons of dried parsley
- ✓ 1 teaspoon of dried thyme
- ✓ 1/4 teaspoon of red pepper flakes, optional
- ✓ 1 lemon, juiced and zested

- ✓ 1 pound of asparagus, trimmed
- ✓ 2 tablespoons of olive oil
- ✓ 4 cups of baby spinach

Step-by-Step Preparation:

1. Preheat the oven to 400°F and line a baking sheet with parchment paper. Season the cod fillets with salt and pepper and place them on one side of the prepared baking sheet.
2. Whisk together the butter, garlic, parsley, thyme, red pepper flakes, lemon juice, and lemon zest in a small bowl. Spoon half of the butter mixture over the cod fillets, reserving the rest for later.
3. Toss the asparagus with the olive oil and season with salt and pepper. Arrange them on the other side of the baking sheet, leaving some space between them.
4. Bake for 15 minutes or until the cod is cooked, flakes easily with a fork, and the asparagus is tender but still crisp.
5. In a large skillet over medium-high heat, wilt the spinach with a splash of water, stirring occasionally, for about 5 minutes or until bright green and soft.
6. Serve the cod fillets with the remaining butter sauce drizzled over them, along with the roasted asparagus and spinach.

Nutritional Facts: (Per serving)

- Calories: 413
- Fat: 24 g
- Carbohydrates: 12 g
- Fiber: 4 g
- Protein: 40 g
- Sodium: 282 mg
- Potassium: 1228 mg
- Calcium: 86 mg
- Iron: 4 mg

This is a simple and satisfying way to enjoy cod, a lean and versatile fish rich in omega-3 fatty acids, vitamin B12, and selenium. The garlic butter sauce adds a burst of flavor and complements the mild taste of the cod. The roasted asparagus and spinach provide antioxidants, vitamin C, and folate. Try this recipe today, and let me know what you think!

Recipe 17: Chicken Skewers With Teriyaki

If you want a low-fat, high-protein, and delicious lunch, try these chicken skewers with teriyaki sauce. They are easy to make and full of flavor. You can marinate the chicken in a homemade teriyaki sauce and grill them until juicy and tender. Serve them with some rice and veggies for a balanced meal. This recipe makes 4 servings and takes about 30 minutes to prepare and cook.

Servings: 4
Prepping Time: 15 minutes
Cook Time: 15 minutes
Difficulty: Easy
Total Time: 30 minutes

☐ **Ingredients:**
- ✓ 1/4 cup of brown sugar
- ✓ 1/4 cup of soy sauce
- ✓ 2 cloves of garlic, minced
- ✓ 1 teaspoon of grated ginger
- ✓ 1 tablespoon of rice vinegar
- ✓ 1 tablespoon of cornstarch
- ✓ 1/4 cup of water
- ✓ 1 pound of chicken breast, cut into bite-sized pieces

✓ 8 wooden skewers, soaked in water for 30 minutes
✓ Optional: sesame seeds and green onions for garnish

Step-by-Step Preparation:
1. Whisk together the brown sugar, soy sauce, garlic, ginger, and rice vinegar in a small saucepan over medium heat. Bring to a boil and then reduce the heat to low.
2. In a small bowl, whisk together the cornstarch and water until smooth. Stir into the saucepan and cook until the sauce is thickened, stirring occasionally, for about 10 minutes.
3. Reserve 1/4 cup of the sauce for later and transfer the rest to a large ziplock bag. Add the chicken pieces and seal the bag. Massage the bag to coat the chicken with the sauce and refrigerate for at least 15 minutes.
4. Preheat a grill to medium-high heat and lightly oil the grate. Thread the chicken pieces onto the skewers, leaving some space between them. Discard the marinade.
5. Grill the chicken skewers for about 15 minutes, turning occasionally, until the chicken is cooked and charred on the edges.
6. Brush the reserved sauce over the chicken skewers and sprinkle with sesame seeds and green onions if desired.
7. Enjoy your chicken skewers with teriyaki sauce!

Nutritional Facts: (Per serving)
- Calories: 262
- Fat: 3 g
- Carbohydrates: 31 g
- Fiber: 0 g
- Protein: 28 g
- Sodium: 1030 mg
- Potassium: 495 mg
- Calcium: 27 mg
- Iron: 1 mg

This is a simple and satisfying way to enjoy chicken with a sweet and savory teriyaki sauce. You can make your sauce with a few ingredients and adjust the sweetness and saltiness to your liking. The chicken skewers are perfect for a quick, leisurely lunch that keeps you full and energized. Try this recipe today, and let me know what you think!

Recipe 18: Canned Tuna Salad With Avocado

This tuna salad is a refreshing and nutritious lunch that is low in fat and protein. It features canned tuna mixed with creamy avocado, crunchy cucumber, onion, spinach, lettuce, and a zesty lime dressing. It's easy to make and serves 4 people. You can enjoy it on its own or with some bread or crackers.

Servings: 4
Prepping Time: 10 minutes
Cook Time: 0 minutes
Difficulty: Easy
Total Time: 10 minutes

Ingredients:
- ✓ 2 (5 oz.) cans of tuna, drained and flaked
- ✓ 1 ripe avocado, peeled and diced
- ✓ 1/4 cup of diced red onion
- ✓ 1/4 cup of chopped fresh cilantro
- ✓ 2 cups of chopped spinach
- ✓ 2 cups of chopped lettuce
- ✓ 1/4 cup of lime juice
- ✓ 2 tablespoons of olive oil

✓ Salt and pepper, to taste

Step-by-Step Preparation:
1. Toss the tuna, avocado, onion, and cilantro in a large bowl.
2. Whisk the lime juice, olive oil, salt, and pepper in a small bowl.
3. Drizzle the dressing over the tuna mixture and toss well to coat.
4. Add the spinach and lettuce and toss lightly to combine.
5. Serve immediately or refrigerate for up to 2 hours.

Nutritional Facts: (Per serving)
- Calories: 272
- Fat: 17 g
- Carbohydrates: 10 g
- Fiber: 5 g
- Protein: 23 g
- Sodium: 246 mg
- Potassium: 637 mg
- Calcium: 51 mg
- Iron: 2 mg

This salad is a great way to use canned tuna and get a boost of omega-3 fatty acids, vitamin C, and folate. The avocado adds a creamy texture and healthy fats, while the cucumber, onion, spinach, and lettuce add crunch and freshness. The lime dressing adds a tangy and bright flavor that complements the tuna. Try this recipe today, and let me know what you think!

Recipe 19: Chicken Shawarma and Hummus

If you love the flavors of chicken shawarma and hummus, you will love this pasta salad that combines them in a delicious and satisfying dish. This recipe is low in fat, high in protein, and perfect for lean lunches. It's easy to make and can be customized with your favorite toppings. Enjoy it cold or warm, with a drizzle of tahini dressing and some fresh herbs.

Servings: 4
Prepping Time: 15 minutes
Cook Time: 20 minutes
Difficulty: Easy
Total Time: 35 minutes

Ingredients:
- ✓ 1 pound of boneless, skinless chicken thighs, sliced thinly
- ✓ 2 tablespoons of shawarma seasoning (see notes for homemade blend)
- ✓ 2 tablespoons of olive oil, divided
- ✓ 8 ounces of whole wheat penne pasta
- ✓ 1/4 cup of hummus
- ✓ 2 tablespoons of lemon juice
- ✓ Salt and pepper, to taste
- ✓ 4 cups of baby spinach

- ✓ 1/4 cup of crumbled feta cheese
- ✓ 1/4 cup of chopped parsley
- ✓ Optional toppings: sliced cherry tomatoes, diced cucumber, sliced red onion, pickled banana peppers, olives, tahini dressing (see notes for recipe)

Step-by-Step Preparation:

1. Toss the chicken with the shawarma seasoning and 1 tablespoon of olive oil in a large ziplock bag. Seal the bag and massage the chicken to coat well. Refrigerate for at least 30 minutes or up to overnight.
2. Cook the pasta according to the package directions until al dente. Drain and rinse under cold water. Transfer to a large bowl and toss with the hummus, lemon juice, salt, pepper, and 1 tablespoon of olive oil. Set aside.
3. Heat a grill pan or a skillet over medium-high heat. Cook the chicken for about 15 minutes, turning occasionally, until charred and cooked. Transfer to a cutting board and let it rest for 5 minutes. Then, chop it into bite-sized pieces.
4. Add the spinach, feta cheese, and parsley to the pasta and toss to combine. Top with the chicken and any optional toppings you like. Drizzle with some tahini dressing if desired. Serve cold or warm, or store in an airtight container in the refrigerator for up to 3 days.

Nutritional Facts: (Per serving)

- Calories: 519
- Fat: 19 g
- Carbohydrates: 54 g
- Fiber: 10 g
- Protein: 37 g

hope you like this recipe. It's a great way to enjoy the flavors of Greek and Middle Eastern cuisine healthily and satisfyingly. Let me know what you think of it.

Recipe 20: Mediterranean Chicken Shawarma

Enjoy the flavors of the Middle East with this easy and healthy chicken shawarma rice bowl. Tender and juicy chicken is marinated in a homemade shawarma spice blend and cooked in a skillet. Then, it is served over fluffy rice with a fresh and crunchy Greek salad, creamy hummus, and salty olives. This recipe is low in fat, high in protein, and perfect for lean lunches. You can make it ahead and store it in the fridge for up to 3 days.

Servings: 4
Prepping Time: 10 minutes
Cook Time: 20 minutes
Difficulty: Easy
Total Time: 30 minutes

Ingredients:
- ✓ 1 pound of boneless, skinless chicken breasts cut into thin strips
- ✓ 2 tablespoons of shawarma seasoning (see notes for homemade blend)
- ✓ 2 tablespoons of olive oil, divided

- ✓ 2 cups of cooked white or brown rice
- ✓ 1/4 cup of hummus
- ✓ 2 cups of chopped romaine lettuce
- ✓ 1 cup of cherry tomatoes, halved
- ✓ 1/2 cup of diced cucumber
- ✓ 1/4 cup of sliced kalamata olives
- ✓ 2 tablespoons of chopped red onion
- ✓ 2 tablespoons of lemon juice
- ✓ 1 teaspoon of dried oregano
- ✓ Salt and pepper, to taste
- ✓ Optional toppings: feta cheese, parsley, tahini sauce

Step-by-Step Preparation:
1. Toss the chicken with the shawarma seasoning and 1 tablespoon of olive oil in a large ziplock bag. Seal the bag and massage the chicken to coat well. Refrigerate for at least 15 minutes or up to overnight.
2. Heat a large skillet over medium-high heat and add 1 tablespoon olive oil. Cook the chicken for about 15 minutes, turning occasionally, until golden and cooked. Transfer to a plate and keep warm.
3. Whisk together the lemon juice, oregano, salt, and pepper in a small bowl. This is the dressing for the salad.
4. Toss the lettuce, tomatoes, cucumber, olives, and onion with the dressing in a large bowl. Adjust the seasoning if needed.
5. To serve, divide the rice among four bowls and top with the chicken, salad, and hummus. Sprinkle with some feta cheese and parsley if desired. Drizzle with some tahini sauce if you like. Enjoy!

☐ **Nutritional Facts: (Per serving)**
- Calories: 424
- Fat: 16 g
- Carbohydrates: 42 g
- Fiber: 5 g
- Protein: 31 g

I hope you like this recipe. It's a great way to enjoy the flavors of the Mediterranean simply and satisfyingly. Let me know what you think of it.

Chapter 04: Refreshing and Nourishing Salad or Soup

Recipe 21: Fresh Quinoa Salad With Vegetables

Quinoa salad with vegetables is delicious and nutritious for a light lunch or a side dish. It is low in fat and protein and packed with fresh and colorful veggies. This recipe is easy to make and can be customized to your taste. You can enjoy it warm or cold; it keeps well in the fridge for up to 3 days.

Servings: **4**
Prepping Time: **15 minutes**
Cook Time: **20 minutes**
Difficulty: **Easy**
Total Time: **35 minutes**

Ingredients:
- ✓ 1 cup quinoa, rinsed and drained
- ✓ 2 cups water

- ✓ Salt and pepper, to taste
- ✓ 1/4 cup olive oil
- ✓ 2 tablespoons lemon juice
- ✓ 1 teaspoon Dijon mustard
- ✓ 1/4 teaspoon garlic powder
- ✓ 2 cups cherry tomatoes, halved
- ✓ 1 cucumber, diced
- ✓ 1/4 cup chopped parsley
- ✓ 1/4 cup chopped mint
- ✓ 1/4 cup feta cheese, crumbled (optional)

Step-by-Step Preparation:
1. Bring the quinoa, water, and a pinch of salt to a boil in a small saucepan. Reduce the heat and simmer, covered, until the quinoa is fluffy and the water is absorbed, about 15 to 20 minutes. Fluff with a fork and transfer to a large bowl.
2. Whisk together the olive oil, lemon juice, mustard, garlic powder, salt, and pepper in a small bowl. This is the dressing for the salad.
3. Add the tomatoes, cucumber, parsley, mint, and feta (if using) to the quinoa. Drizzle the dressing over the salad and toss to combine.
4. Serve the salad warm or cold, or refrigerate for later.

Nutritional Facts: (Per serving)
- Calories: **354**
- Fat: **19 g**
- Carbohydrates: **40 g**
- Fiber: **6 g**
- Protein: **10 g**

Quinoa salad with vegetables is a healthy and satisfying meal you can whip up quickly. It is full of flavor, texture, and nutrients and great for meal prep or picnics. You can also add other ingredients to make it your own, such as olives, nuts, beans, or chicken. Enjoy this quinoa salad with vegetables, and let me know what you think!

Recipe 22: Healthy Kale and Lentil Soup

Homemade kale and lentil soup is a warm, comforting dish that is easy to make and good for you. It is low in fat, high in protein, and rich in fiber and iron. This soup is vegan, gluten-free, and dairy-free, but you can customize it to your liking. You can enjoy it as a main course or a side dish, and it freezes well for later use.

Servings: **4**
Prepping Time: **10 minutes**
Cook Time: **40 minutes**
Difficulty: **Easy**
Total Time: **50 minutes**

Ingredients:
- ✓ 1 tablespoon of olive oil
- ✓ 1 onion, chopped
- ✓ 2 carrots, peeled and diced
- ✓ 2 celery stalks, diced
- ✓ 4 garlic cloves, minced

- ✓ 1 teaspoon of cumin
- ✓ 1 teaspoon of curry powder
- ✓ 1/4 teaspoon of red pepper flakes
- ✓ Salt and pepper, to taste
- ✓ 4 cups of vegetable broth
- ✓ 4 cups of water
- ✓ 1 vegetable bouillon cube
- ✓ 1 cup of green or brown lentils, rinsed and drained
- ✓ 4 cups of kale, stemmed and chopped
- ✓ 2 tablespoons of lemon juice

Step-by-Step Preparation:

1. Heat the oil in a large pot over medium-high heat. Add the onion, carrot, celery, and garlic and cook, stirring occasionally, until soft, about 15 minutes.
2. Add the cumin, curry powder, red pepper flakes, salt, and pepper and cook, stirring, for another minute.
3. Add the broth, water, bouillon cube, and lentils and boil. Reduce the heat and simmer, partially covered, until the lentils are tender, about 25 minutes.
4. Stir in the kale and lemon juice and cook until the kale is wilted about 5 minutes.
5. Enjoy your homemade kale and lentil soup, or let it cool and store it in an airtight container in the refrigerator for up to 4 days or in the freezer for up to 3 months.

Nutritional Facts: (Per serving)

- Calories: **295**
- Fat: **6 g**
- Carbohydrates: **47 g**
- Fiber: **18 g**
- Protein: **17 g**

Homemade kale and lentil soup is a hearty and healthy meal you can make in less than an hour. It is full of flavor, texture, and nutrients and is excellent for cold days or when you need an energy boost. You can also add other ingredients, such as potatoes, mushrooms, spinach, or cheese, to make it your own. Enjoy this homemade kale and lentil soup, and let me know what you think!

Recipe 23: Cucumber Tuna Avocado Salad

Cucumber tuna avocado salad is a refreshing and satisfying dish for a hot summer day. It is low in fat, high in protein, and loaded with healthy fats and antioxidants. This recipe is straightforward to make and requires no cooking. You can enjoy it as a light meal or a side dish; it keeps well in the fridge for up to 2 days.

Servings: **4**
Prepping Time: **10 minutes**
Cook Time: **0 minutes**
Difficulty: **Easy**
Total Time: **10 minutes**

Ingredients:
- ✓ 2 cans of tuna, drained and flaked
- ✓ 2 ripe avocados, peeled and diced
- ✓ 1 large cucumber, diced
- ✓ 1/4 cup of red onion, thinly sliced
- ✓ 2 tablespoons of fresh lemon juice
- ✓ 2 tablespoons of olive oil
- ✓ Salt and pepper, to taste
- ✓ 2 tablespoons of chopped parsley or cilantro for garnish

Step-by-Step Preparation:
1. Toss the tuna, avocado, cucumber, and onion in a large bowl.
2. Whisk the lemon juice, olive oil, salt, and pepper in a small bowl. This is the dressing for the salad.
3. Drizzle the sauce over the salad and toss to coat.
4. Sprinkle the parsley or cilantro over the salad and serve, or refrigerate until ready to eat.

Nutritional Facts: (Per serving)
- Calories: **358**
- Fat: **23 g**
- Carbohydrates: **17 g**
- Fiber: **9 g**
- Protein: **26 g**

Cucumber tuna avocado salad is a delicious and nutritious way to enjoy the fresh flavors of summer. It is full of protein, healthy fats, and vitamins and is excellent for skin and hair. You can customize it by adding other ingredients such as tomatoes, olives, corn, or cheese. Enjoy this cucumber tuna avocado salad, and let me know what you think!

Recipe 24: Healthy Mango and Prawn Salad

If you are looking for a refreshing and nutritious summer salad, look no further than this healthy mango and prawn salad. It is a low-fat, high-protein dish that combines juicy prawns, sweet mangoes, creamy avocado, crunchy vegetables, and a zesty lime dressing. It is easy to make, ready in 15 minutes, and perfect for a light lunch or dinner. You can also serve it with rice, noodles, or bread for a more filling meal.

Servings: **4**
Prepping Time: **10 minutes**
Cook Time: **5 minutes**
Difficulty: **Easy**
Total Time: **15 minutes**

Ingredients:
- ✓ 400 g cooked prawns, peeled and chopped
- ✓ 2 ripe mangoes, peeled and diced
- ✓ 1 large avocado, peeled and sliced
- ✓ 200 g cherry tomatoes, halved
- ✓ 100 g baby spinach leaves
- ✓ 1/4 red onion, thinly sliced
- ✓ 2 tbsp chopped fresh parsley

✓ 2 tbsp chopped fresh chives
✓ 50 g feta cheese, crumbled
✓ Salt and pepper, to taste

For the dressing:
- 1/4 cup olive oil
- 1/4 cup fresh lime juice
- 1 garlic clove, minced
- 1 tsp honey
- 1/4 tsp salt
- 1/4 tsp black pepper
- A pinch of chili flakes, optional

Step-by-Step Preparation:
1. Whisk together all the dressing ingredients in a small bowl until well combined. Set aside.
2. Toss the prawns, mangoes, avocado, cherry tomatoes, spinach, onion, parsley, and chives in a large bowl. Season with salt and pepper to taste.
3. Drizzle the dressing over the salad and toss gently to coat. Sprinkle the feta cheese on top.
4. Serve immediately or refrigerate until ready to serve. Enjoy!

Nutritional Facts (Per serving):
- Calories: **440**
- Fat: **27 g**
- Carbohydrates: **31 g**
- Fiber: **7 g**
- Protein: **25 g**

This healthy mango and prawn salad is a delicious way to enjoy the fresh flavors of summer. It is packed with protein, vitamins, minerals, and antioxidants to energize and satisfy you. You can customize it with your favorite vegetables, herbs, cheese, or nuts. It is also gluten-free, dairy-free, and low-carb. Try it today, and let me know what you think!

Recipe 25: Winter Vegetable Detox Soup

This winter detox soup of lentils is a hearty and warming dish that will help you cleanse your body and boost your immune system. It is loaded with vegetables, spices, and herbs that have anti-inflammatory and antioxidant properties. It is also low in fat and protein, making it a satisfying and balanced meal. You can make this soup in a crockpot or on the stovetop and enjoy it with some crusty bread or a green salad.

Servings: **4**
Prepping Time: **15 minutes**
Cook Time: **40 minutes (crockpot) or 20 minutes (stovetop)**
Difficulty: **Easy**
Total Time: **55 minutes (crockpot) or 35 minutes (stovetop)**

Ingredients:
- ✓ 1 tbsp olive oil
- ✓ 1 onion, chopped
- ✓ 2 garlic cloves, minced
- ✓ 2 carrots, peeled and diced
- ✓ 2 celery stalks, diced
- ✓ 1 tsp salt
- ✓ 1/4 tsp black pepper

- ✓ 1 tsp turmeric
- ✓ 1/2 tsp cumin
- ✓ 1/4 tsp chili flakes, optional
- ✓ 4 cups vegetable broth
- ✓ 1 cup green lentils, rinsed and drained
- ✓ 1/4 cup chopped fresh parsley
- ✓ 2 tbsp lemon juice

Step-by-Step Preparation:

1. If using a crockpot, heat the oil in a skillet over medium-high heat. Add the onion, garlic, carrots, celery, salt, pepper, turmeric, cumin, and chili flakes, if using, and cook, stirring occasionally, for about 10 minutes, until the onion is soft and the spices are fragrant. Transfer the mixture to the crockpot.
2. Heat the oil in a large pot over medium-high heat if using a stovetop. Add the onion, garlic, carrots, celery, salt, pepper, turmeric, cumin, and chili flakes, if using, and cook, stirring occasionally, for about 10 minutes, until the onion is soft and the spices are fragrant.
3. Add the broth and lentils to the crockpot or the pot and stir to combine. Cover and cook on low for 40 minutes (crockpot) or bring to a boil and then reduce the heat and simmer for 20 minutes (stovetop) until the lentils are tender.
4. Stir in the parsley and lemon juice, and adjust the seasoning if needed. Serve hot, garnished with more parsley if desired.

Nutritional Facts (Per serving):

- Calories: **260**
- Fat: **5 g**
- Carbohydrates: **40 g**
- Fiber: **16 g**
- Protein: **15 g**

This winter detox soup of lentils is a simple and delicious way to nourish your body and soul. It is packed with flavor, texture, and nutrients to help you feel energized and refreshed. You can store the leftovers in an airtight container in the refrigerator for up to 3 days or freeze them for up to 3 months. Enjoy this soup as a cozy and comforting meal on a cold day or as a part of a detox plan.

Recipe 26: Caprese Salad With Horse Meat

This Caprese salad with horse meat, tenderloin, salamis, cheese, and tomatoes is a unique and delicious twist on the classic Italian dish. It is a low fat, high-protein salad with tender slices of horse meat, creamy salakis cheese juicy cherry tomatoes, and fresh basil leaves. It is drizzled with a simple balsamic dressing that enhances the flavors of the ingredients. It is a quick and easy dish that can be served as a main course or a side dish.

Servings: **4**
Prepping Time: **10 minutes**
Cook Time: **10 minutes**
Difficulty: **Easy**
Total Time: **20 minutes**

Ingredients:
- ✓ 400 g horse meat tenderloin, trimmed and cut into thin slices
- ✓ Salt and pepper, to taste
- ✓ 2 tbsp olive oil
- ✓ 200 g salaries cheese, cut into small cubes
- ✓ 300 g cherry tomatoes, halved
- ✓ 1/4 cup fresh basil leaves, torn
- ✓ 2 tbsp balsamic vinegar

✓ 1 tsp honey
✓ A pinch of chili flakes, optional

Step-by-Step Preparation:
1. Season the horse meat slices with salt and pepper on both sides. Heat the oil in a large skillet over high heat. Cook the meat for about 2 minutes per side or until browned and cooked to your liking. Transfer to a plate and keep warm.
2. Whisk together the balsamic vinegar, honey, and chili flakes in a small bowl. Set aside.
3. Arrange the salami cheese, cherry tomatoes, and basil leaves on a large platter. Sprinkle with some salt and pepper, if desired.
4. Top with the horse meat slices and drizzle with the balsamic dressing. Serve hot or cold, as you prefer.

Nutritional Facts (Per serving):
- Calories: **420**
- Fat: **22 g**
- Carbohydrates: **15 g**
- Fiber: **2 g**
- Protein: **42 g**

This Caprese salad with horse meat, tenderloin, salamis, cheese, and tomatoes is a mouthwatering and nutritious dish that will impress your guests. It is also a good iron, zinc, and vitamin B12 source. You can pair this salad with crusty bread, pasta, or rice for a complete meal. Bon appetit!

Recipe 27: Italian Tortellini Soup With Vegetables

This soup is a hearty and delicious meal that combines tender cheese tortellini, nutty wild rice, and colorful vegetables in a creamy tomato broth. It's easy to make and low in fat and protein. Add some cooked chicken or turkey for extra flavor and texture. This recipe serves 4 people and is ready in less than an hour.

Servings: 4
Prepping Time: 15 minutes
Cook Time: 35 minutes
Difficulty: Easy
Total Time: 50 minutes

Ingredients:
- ✓ 1 tablespoon of olive oil
- ✓ 1 onion, chopped
- ✓ 2 garlic cloves, minced
- ✓ 2 carrots, peeled and sliced
- ✓ 2 celery stalks, diced
- ✓ 4 cups of vegetable broth

- ✓ 1 (14.5 oz) can of diced tomatoes, undrained
- ✓ 1/4 teaspoon of dried rosemary
- ✓ Salt and pepper, to taste
- ✓ 1 cup of wild rice blend, rinsed
- ✓ 1 (9 oz) package of refrigerated cheese tortellini
- ✓ 2 cups of baby spinach, chopped
- ✓ 1/4 cup of heavy cream
- ✓ Grated Parmesan cheese for serving

Step-by-Step Preparation:

1. Heat the oil in a large pot over medium-high heat and sauté the onion, garlic, carrots, and celery for about 10 minutes, stirring occasionally, until soft.
2. Add the broth, tomatoes, rosemary, salt, and pepper, and boil. Reduce the heat and simmer for 15 minutes.
3. Stir in the rice and tortellini and cook for 15 to 20 minutes or until the rice and pasta are tender.
4. Stir in the spinach and cream and cook for another 5 minutes, until the spinach is wilted.
5. Ladle the soup into bowls and sprinkle with Parmesan cheese. Enjoy!

Nutritional Facts: (Per serving)

- Calories: 520
- Fat: 18 g
- Carbohydrates: 72 g
- Fiber: 8 g
- Protein: 19 g

This creamy Italian tortellini wild rice soup with vegetables is a perfect way to warm up on a cold day. It's filling, satisfying, and full of flavor. You can customize it with your favorite vegetables, herbs, and cheese. It's a great dish to make and reheat later or freeze for future meals. Try it today and see for yourself how delicious it is!

Recipe 28: Greek Salad Fresh Cucumber

Experience the refreshing taste of the Mediterranean with this Greek salad. It's a low-fat, high-protein dish perfect for a light lunch or dinner, packed with fresh cucumber, tomato, sweet pepper, lettuce, red onion, feta cheese, and olives.

Servings: 4 people
Prepping Time: 15 minutes
Cook Time: 0 minutes
Difficulty: Easy
Total Time: 15 minutes

Ingredients:
- ✓ 2 cucumbers
- ✓ 4 tomatoes
- ✓ 2 sweet peppers
- ✓ 1 head of lettuce
- ✓ 1 red onion

- ✓ 200g feta cheese
- ✓ 1 cup of olives
- ✓ Olive oil for dressing

Step-by-Step Preparation:
1. Chop all the vegetables and cheese into bite-sized pieces.
2. Mix them in a large bowl.
3. Drizzle with olive oil and toss until everything is well coated.

Nutritional Facts: (Per serving)
- Calories: 200
- Protein: 8g
- Fat: 14g (Saturated: 6g)
- Carbohydrates: 10g (Fiber: 3g, Sugars: 6g)

Enjoy this Greek salad as a standalone meal, or pair it with a warm soup for a satisfying and healthy meal. It's a great way to incorporate more vegetables into your diet while enjoying a burst of flavors from the Mediterranean.

Recipe 29: Healthy Chicken Orzo Salad

If you are looking for a low-fat, high-protein salad and soup dish, you will love this homemade chicken orzo salad with peppers and feta. It is easy to make, colorful, and full of Mediterranean flavors. You can enjoy it warm or cold, as a main course or as a side dish. It is perfect for a family meal or a potluck.

Servings: 4
Prepping Time: 15 minutes
Cook Time: 15 minutes
Difficulty: Easy
Total Time: 30 minutes
Ingredients:
- ✓ 1/4 cup of basil pesto
- ✓ 2 tablespoons of balsamic vinegar
- ✓ 1 pound of chicken tenders
- ✓ Salt and pepper, to taste
- ✓ 8 ounces of orzo pasta
- ✓ 4 cups of chicken broth
- ✓ 1/4 cup of olive oil
- ✓ 3 tablespoons of lemon juice
- ✓ 2 teaspoons of honey

- ✓ 1 teaspoon of dried oregano
- ✓ 1/4 teaspoon of garlic powder
- ✓ 2 cups of cherry tomatoes, halved
- ✓ 1/4 cup of sliced black olives
- ✓ 1/4 cup of chopped roasted red peppers
- ✓ 1/4 cup of crumbled feta cheese
- ✓ 2 tablespoons of chopped fresh parsley

Step-by-Step Preparation:

1. In a small bowl, whisk together the pesto and vinegar. Season the chicken tenders with salt and pepper and coat them with the pesto mixture. Set aside for 10 minutes to marinate.
2. In a large pot, bring the chicken broth to a boil. Add the orzo and cook, stirring occasionally, until al dente, about 10 to 12 minutes. Drain and return to the pot.
3. Whisk together the olive oil, lemon juice, honey, oregano, garlic powder, salt, and pepper in another small bowl. Pour over the orzo and toss to combine.
4. Heat a grill pan over medium-high heat. Grill the chicken tenders for about 4 minutes per side or until cooked through and charred. Cut into bite-sized pieces and add to the orzo.
5. Add the tomatoes, olives, peppers, feta, and parsley to the orzo and chicken. Toss gently to combine.
6. Serve warm or cold, or refrigerate for later.

Nutritional Facts: (Per serving)

- Calories: 638
- Fat: 28 g
- Carbohydrates: 62 g
- Protein: 38 g
- Fiber: 4 g
- Sugar: 12 g
- Sodium: 1030 mg
- Cholesterol: 95 mg

This homemade chicken orzo salad with peppers and feta is a delicious and nutritious dish you can make in 30 minutes. It is packed with protein, fiber, and antioxidants and has a tangy and savory dressing that complements the fresh and roasted vegetables. You can serve it as a salad or a soup, depending on your preference. It is a great way to use leftover chicken or pesto, and it keeps well in the fridge for up to 3 days. Enjoy!

Recipe 30: Delicious Crusted Salmon

Crusted salmon and baroa mashed potatoes are low-fat, high-protein salad and soup dishes that are easy to make and delicious. You will love the crispy potato crust on the tender salmon fillets and the creamy and fluffy baroa mashed potatoes that go along with it. Baroa is a sweet potato with yellow-orange flesh and a nutty flavor. It is rich in vitamin A, fiber, and antioxidants. This dish is perfect for a cozy and satisfying meal.

Servings: 4
Prepping Time: 15 minutes
Cook Time: 25 minutes
Difficulty: Easy
Total Time: 40 minutes

Ingredients:
- ✓ 4 salmon fillets, about 6 ounces each
- ✓ Salt and pepper, to taste
- ✓ 2 tablespoons of whole-grain mustard
- ✓ 2 cups of shredded potatoes, squeezed dry
- ✓ 2 tablespoons of olive oil
- ✓ 4 barra potatoes, peeled and cut into chunks
- ✓ 4 tablespoons of butter

✓ 1/4 cup of milk
✓ 2 tablespoons of chopped fresh parsley
✓ 4 cups of chicken or vegetable broth
✓ Sour cream for serving (optional)

Step-by-Step Preparation:
1. Preheat oven to 375°F and line a baking sheet with parchment paper. Season the salmon fillets with salt and pepper and spread the mustard evenly over the top of each fillet. Press the shredded potatoes onto the mustard to form a crust. Place the fillets on the prepared baking sheet and drizzle with 1 tablespoon of olive oil. Bake for 15 to 20 minutes or until the salmon is cooked and the potato crust is golden and crisp.
2. Meanwhile, in a large pot, bring the baroa potatoes and enough water to cover them to a boil. Cook for 15 to 20 minutes or until the potatoes are very tender. Drain and return to the pot. Add the butter, milk, parsley, salt, and pepper and mash with a potato masher or an electric mixer until smooth and creamy.
3. In a small saucepan, bring the broth to a boil and simmer until slightly reduced about 10 minutes.
4. To serve, divide the baron mashed potatoes among four plates and top with a salmon fillet. Spoon some broth over the dish and garnish with sour cream if desired.

Nutritional Facts: (Per serving)
- Calories: 667
- Fat: 34 g
- Carbohydrates: 49 g
- Protein: 43 g
- Fiber: 6 g
- Sugar: 11 g
- Sodium: 713 mg
- Cholesterol: 121 mg

This crusted salmon and baroa mashed potatoes recipe is a great way to enjoy a hearty and healthy meal. The salmon provides omega-3 fatty acids, the baron potatoes provide vitamin A and fiber, and the broth adds flavor and hydration. You can customize this dish using different types of potatoes, mustard, or broth. Enjoy!

Chapter 05: Poultry And Meat Without The Fat

Recipe 31: Roast Chicken With Lemon

Roast chicken with lemon and honey glaze is a low-fat, high-protein poultry and meat dish that is simple to make and delicious. You will love the juicy, tender chicken with a crispy, sweet crust flavored with garlic, mustard, and spices. This dish is perfect for a cozy and satisfying meal with your family or friends.

Servings: 4
Prepping Time: 10 minutes
Cook Time: 45 minutes
Difficulty: Easy
Total Time: 55 minutes

Ingredients:
- ✓ 1/4 cup of honey
- ✓ 2 tablespoons of lemon juice

- ✓ 2 teaspoons of minced garlic
- ✓ 1 teaspoon of Dijon mustard
- ✓ 1/2 teaspoon of paprika
- ✓ 1/4 teaspoon of cayenne pepper
- ✓ Salt and black pepper, to taste
- ✓ 4 chicken breasts, about 6 ounces each, with skin and bone
- ✓ 4 sprigs of fresh thyme

Step-by-Step Preparation:

1. Preheat the oven to 425°F and line a baking sheet with parchment paper. Whisk together the honey, lemon juice, garlic, mustard, paprika, and cayenne in a small bowl. Season the chicken breasts with salt and pepper and place them on the prepared baking sheet. Tuck a thyme sprig under the skin of each breast.
2. Roast the chicken for 30 minutes, basting with the honey mixture every 10 minutes. Increase the oven temperature to 450°F and roast for another 15 minutes until the chicken is cooked and the skin is golden and crisp.
3. Transfer the chicken to a platter and let it rest for 10 minutes. Drizzle with the pan juices and serve.

Nutritional Facts: (Per serving)

- Calories: 353
- Fat: 11 g
- Carbohydrates: 23 g
- Protein: 42 g
- Fiber: 0 g
- Sugar: 22 g
- Sodium: 269 mg
- Cholesterol: 124 mg

This roast chicken with lemon and honey glaze recipe is a great way to enjoy hearty and healthy meal. The chicken is moist and flavorful, and the glaze adds a touch of sweetness and spice. You can customize this dish using different herbs, spices, or citrus juices. Enjoy!

Recipe 32: Grilled Buffalo Chicken Breasts

Grilled buffalo chicken breasts are a low-fat, high-protein poultry and mea dish that is easy to make and delicious. You will love the spicy, tangy buffalo sauce that coats the juicy and tender chicken. This dish is perfect for a quicl and satisfying meal with your family or friends.

Servings: 4
Prepping Time: 10 minutes
Cook Time: 15 minutes
Difficulty: Easy
Total Time: 25 minutes

Ingredients:
- ✓ 4 boneless, skinless chicken breasts
- ✓ 1/4 cup of ranch dressing mix
- ✓ 1/2 cup of buffalo hot sauce (such as Frank's RedHot)
- ✓ Crumbled blue cheese for serving (optional)
- ✓ Chopped green onion for garnish (optional)
- ✓ Ranch or blue cheese dressing for dipping (optional)

Step-by-Step Preparation:
1. Place the chicken breasts, ranch dressing mix, and buffalo sauce in a large ziplock bag. Seal the bag and massage the chicken to coat with the sauce. Refrigerate for at least one hour or up to overnight.
2. Preheat the grill to medium-high heat and oil the grates. Remove the chicken from the bag and discard the marinade. Grill the chicken for 6 to 8 minutes per side or until the internal temperature reaches 165°F.
3. Transfer the chicken to a platter and sprinkle with blue cheese and green onion if desired. Serve with ranch or blue cheese dressing for dipping if desired.

Nutritional Facts: (Per serving)
- Calories: 243
- Fat: 7 g
- Carbohydrates: 6 g
- Protein: 38 g
- Fiber: 0 g
- Sugar: 3 g
- Sodium: 1130 mg
- Cholesterol: 98 mg

This grilled buffalo chicken breasts recipe is a great way to enjoy a hearty and healthy meal. The chicken is moist and flavorful, and the buffalo sauce adds a kick of heat and vinegar. You can customize this dish using hot sauces, cheese, or dressings. Enjoy!

Recipe 33: Beef and Snowpeas Stirfry

You are looking for a recipe for Chinese beef and snowpeas stirfry stir fry. This delicious and easy dish can be made in less than 30 minutes. It features tender beef slices and crunchy snow peas in a savory and slightly sweet sauce. Here is a possible recipe for you:

Servings: 4
Prepping Time: 15 minutes
Cook Time: 10 minutes
Difficulty: Easy
Total Time: 25 minutes

Ingredients:
- ✓ 1 pound beef steak or tenderloin, thinly sliced
- ✓ 2 tablespoons soy sauce
- ✓ 1 tablespoon oyster sauce
- ✓ 1/2 teaspoon sugar
- ✓ 1/4 teaspoon salt
- ✓ 2 teaspoons corn starch, divided
- ✓ 1 teaspoon sesame oil
- ✓ 1/4 cup vegetable oil
- ✓ 2 garlic cloves, minced

- ✓ 8 slices fresh ginger
- ✓ 1 cup snow peas, ends trimmed
- ✓ 1 teaspoon dark soy sauce
- ✓ 1/4 cup water

Step-by-Step Preparation:

1. Combine the beef slices, soy sauce, oyster sauce, sugar, salt, 1 teaspoon of cornstarch, and sesame oil in a large bowl. Mix well and marinate in the refrigerator for at least 15 minutes.
2. Whisk together the dark soy sauce, water, and 1 teaspoon of cornstarch in a small bowl. Set aside.
3. Heat the oil over high heat until smoking in a wok or large skillet. Add the garlic and ginger and stirfry for 30 seconds or until fragrant.
4. Add the beef and stirfry for 2 minutes or until browned. Transfer to a plate and keep warm.
5. Add the snow peas and stirfry in the same wok for 3 minutes or until crisp-tender. Season with a pinch of salt if needed.
6. Return the beef to the wok and pour in the sauce. Stirfry for another minute or until the sauce is thickened and coats the beef and snow peas.
7. Serve hot with steamed rice or noodles.

Nutritional Facts: (Per serving)

- Calories: 380
- Fat: 24 g
- Carbohydrates: 9 g
- Protein: 32 g
- Sodium: 900 mg

This recipe is adapted from and. You can also check out another variation. I hope you enjoy this dish and have a wonderful day!

Recipe 34: Herb-Marinated Grilled Turkey Meatloaf

Turkey meatloaf is a delicious and healthy alternative to traditional beef. It's moist, flavorful, and easy to make with simple ingredients. This recipe serves four people and is perfect for a cozy family dinner or a meal prep option. Enjoy it with mashed potatoes, green beans, or your favorite side dish.

Servings: 4
Prepping Time: 15 minutes
Cook Time: 1-hour
Difficulty: Easy
Total Time: 1 hour 15 minutes

Ingredients:
- ✓ 1 1/4 pounds ground turkey (93% lean)
- ✓ 1/2 cup panko breadcrumbs
- ✓ 1/4 cup milk
- ✓ 1 large egg
- ✓ 1/4 cup onion, finely chopped

- ✓ 2 cloves garlic, minced
- ✓ 2 teaspoons Worcestershire sauce
- ✓ 1 teaspoon salt
- ✓ 1/2 teaspoon black pepper
- ✓ 1/4 cup ketchup
- ✓ 2 tablespoons brown sugar

Step-by-Step Preparation:

1. Preheat oven to 375°F and lightly grease a baking sheet.
2. In a large bowl, combine turkey, breadcrumbs, milk, egg, onion, garlic, Worcestershire sauce, salt, and pepper. Mix well with your hands until well combined.
3. Shape the mixture into a loaf on the prepared baking sheet.
4. In a small bowl, whisk together ketchup and brown sugar. Brush the mixture over the top and sides of the meatloaf.
5. Bake for 50 to 60 minutes or until a thermometer inserted in the center reads 165°F.
6. Let the meatloaf rest for 10 minutes before slicing and serving.

Nutritional Facts: (Per serving)

- Calories: 330
- Fat: 12 g
- Carbohydrates: 25 g
- Protein: 32 g
- Fiber: 1 g
- Sodium: 660 mg

This turkey meatloaf is a satisfying and nutritious meal everyone will love. It's low in fat and protein, making it an excellent choice for a balanced diet. You can store the leftovers in an airtight container in the refrigerator for up to 4 days or in the freezer for up to 3 months. Reheat in the oven or microwave, and enjoy!

Recipe 35: BBQ Roast Bratwurst Sausages

You will enjoy this BBQ roast Bratwurst recipe if you love German sausages. It is a low-fat, high-protein dish that is easy to make and perfect for summer barbecue. You can serve it with your favorite sides, such as potato salad, coleslaw, or sauerkraut. This recipe makes 4 servings to share with your family or friends.

Servings: 4
Prepping Time: 10 minutes
Cook Time: 20 minutes
Difficulty: Easy
Total Time: 30 minutes

Ingredients:
- ✓ 4 fresh Bratwurst sausages
- ✓ 1/4 cup of barbecue sauce
- ✓ 4 buns or rolls
- ✓ Optional toppings: mustard, sauerkraut, relish, etc.

Step-by-Step Preparation:

1. Preheat your grill to medium-high heat and oil the grates lightly.
2. Place the Bratwurst sausages on the indirect side of the grill and close the lid. Cook for about 15 minutes, turning occasionally, until the internal temperature reaches 160°F.
3. Brush the sausages with barbecue sauce and move them to the direct side of the grill. Cook for another 5 minutes, turning and basting with more sauce, until they are charred and sticky.
4. Transfer the sausages to a platter and let them rest for 5 minutes.
5. Toast the buns or rolls on the grill, if desired.
6. Serve the sausages on the buns or rolls with your preferred toppings.

Nutritional Facts: (Per serving)
- Calories: 462
- Fat: 26 g
- Carbohydrates: 34 g
- Protein: 22 g
- Sodium: 1010 mg
- Sugar: 11 g

I hope you enjoy this BBQ roast Bratwurst recipe. It is a delicious way to enjoy German sausages with a smoky and sweet flavor. You can adjust the amount of barbecue sauce and toppings to your liking. This dish is excellent for a casual and fun meal with your loved ones. Let me know how it turns out for you.

Recipe 36: Beef and Broccoli American Stir-Fry

You'll love this easy and delicious beef and broccoli stir-fry if you love Chinese takeout. It's a classic dish that pairs tender beef slices with crisp broccoli florets in a savory sauce. You can make it in less than 30 minutes with simple ingredients and enjoy it with steamed rice or noodles. It's a low-fat, high-protein meal that satisfies your cravings and nourishes your body.

Servings: 4
Prepping Time: 15 minutes
Cook Time: 15 minutes
Difficulty: Easy
Total Time: 30 minutes

Ingredients:
- ✓ 1/2 pound sirloin steak, thinly sliced against the grain
- ✓ 2 teaspoons soy sauce, divided
- ✓ 2 teaspoons cornstarch, divided
- ✓ 4 cups broccoli florets
- ✓ 2 tablespoons vegetable oil
- ✓ 2 cloves garlic, minced
- ✓ 1 teaspoon ginger, grated
- ✓ 1/2 cup water
- ✓ 1 tablespoon oyster sauce

✓ 1/2 teaspoon sesame oil
✓ 1 teaspoon brown sugar
✓ Salt, to taste

Step-by-Step Preparation:
1. In a small bowl, toss the beef with 2 teaspoons of soy sauce and 2 teaspoons of cornstarch. Let it marinate for 15 minutes at room temperature.
2. In a pot of boiling water, blanch the broccoli for 2 minutes, then drain and rinse under cold water. Set aside.
3. whisk together the water, oyster sauce, sesame oil, brown sugar, and the remaining soy sauce and cornstarch in a small bowl. Set aside.
4. Heat a wok or large skillet over high heat and add the oil. Add the beef and stir-fry for about 4 minutes when the oil is hot or until browned. Transfer to a plate and keep warm.
5. In the same wok, add the garlic and ginger and stir-fry for 30 seconds or until fragrant. Add the broccoli and the sauce and bring to a boil. Cook, stirring, until the sauce is thickened and the broccoli is coated about 2 minutes.
6. Return the beef to the wok and toss to combine. Season with salt if needed. Serve hot with rice or noodles.

Nutritional Facts: (Per serving)
- Calories: 224
- Fat: 11 g
- Carbohydrates: 13 g
- Protein: 19 g
- Fiber: 3 g
- Sodium: 443 mg

Enjoy this easy and tasty beef and broccoli stir-fry at home and save yourself a trip to the restaurant. It's a great way to use leftover meat or broccoli in the fridge. You can customize the sauce to your liking by adding more or less sugar, soy sauce, or oyster sauce. This dish will become a family favorite you'll make again and again.

Recipe 37: Grilled Chicken Thighs

If you want a low-fat, high-protein, and delicious dish, try these grilled chicken thighs with spices and lemon. They are marinated in a zesty and aromatic mixture of lemon juice, garlic, Dijon mustard, oregano, and thyme, then grilled until juicy and charred. Serve them with a fresh salad, roasted potatoes, or rice for a satisfying meal.

Servings: 4
Prepping Time: 10 minutes
Cook Time: 20 minutes
Difficulty: Easy
Total Time: 30 minutes

Ingredients:
- ✓ 1/4 cup of lemon juice
- ✓ 2 tablespoons of olive oil
- ✓ 4 cloves of garlic, minced
- ✓ 2 teaspoons of Dijon mustard
- ✓ 1 teaspoon of dried oregano
- ✓ 1/2 teaspoon of dried thyme
- ✓ Salt and pepper, to taste
- ✓ 8 boneless, skinless chicken thighs

✓ Lemon wedges for serving

Step-by-Step Preparation:

. whisk together the lemon juice, olive oil, garlic, Dijon, oregano, thyme, salt, and pepper in a small bowl. Pour the marinade over the chicken thighs n a large ziplock bag or a shallow dish. Seal or cover and refrigerate for at east 2 hours or overnight.

. Preheat a grill or a grill pan over medium-high heat. Remove the chicken rom the marinade and discard the excess. Grill the chicken for 10 minutes per side until cooked through and slightly charred. Transfer to a platter and et rest for 5 minutes.

. Serve the chicken with lemon wedges and your choice of sides. Enjoy!

Nutritional Facts: (Per serving)
- Calories: 287
- Fat: 15 g
- Carbohydrates: 3 g
- Protein: 35 g

hope you like this recipe. You can adjust the seasonings and the cooking ime according to your preference. This dish is perfect for a summer barbecue or a cozy dinner. Thank you for using Bing. Have a nice day!

Recipe 38: Baked Chicken Tenders

You will love these crunchy baked chicken tenders if you are looking for low-fat, high-protein, and delicious dish. They are coated with cornflakes and panko breadcrumbs, seasoned with garlic and paprika, and baked until golden and crispy. They are perfect for dipping in your favorite sauce or enjoying as they are.

Servings: 4
Prepping Time: 10 minutes
Cook Time: 20 minutes
Difficulty: Easy
Total Time: 30 minutes

Ingredients
- ✓ 1 pound of chicken tenders
- ✓ Salt and pepper, to taste
- ✓ 1/4 cup of all-purpose flour
- ✓ 2 eggs, lightly beaten
- ✓ 1 cup of cornflake crumbs
- ✓ 1/2 cup of panko breadcrumbs
- ✓ 1 teaspoon of garlic powder
- ✓ 1/2 teaspoon of paprika

✓ Cooking spray or oil

Step-by-Step Preparation

1. Preheat oven to 200°C (400°F) and line a baking sheet with parchment paper.
2. Season chicken tenders with salt and pepper on both sides.
3. Place flour in a shallow dish, eggs in another, cornflake crumbs, panko breadcrumbs, garlic powder, and paprika in a third shallow dish. Mix well to combine the crumbs and spices.
4. Dredge each chicken tender in flour, shaking off any excess, then dip in eggs, letting any excess drip off, then coat with the crumb mixture, pressing gently to adhere. Place on the prepared baking sheet and repeat with the remaining chicken tenders.
5. Spray or drizzle the chicken tenders with some cooking spray or oil, and bake for 15 to 20 minutes, flipping halfway through, until golden and cooked through.
6. Serve hot with your favorite dipping sauce, or enjoy as they are.

Nutritional Facts (Per serving)

- Calories: 287
- Fat: 7 g
- Carbohydrates: 27 g
- Protein: 29 g
- Sodium: 331 mg
- Fiber: 1 g
- Sugar: 3 g

These crunchy baked chicken tenders are a family-friendly and satisfying meal you can make in less than an hour. They are tender, juicy, and flavorful, and you can customize them with your favorite spices and sauces. They are also great for meal prep, as you can store them in an airtight container in the refrigerator for up to 3 days or in the freezer for up to 3 months. To reheat, bake them in the oven until warm and crisp. Enjoy!

Recipe 39: Chicken Chickpea Vegetable

If you want a hearty, healthy, and delicious meal, try this chicken chickpea vegetable recipe. It is easy to make in one pan with simple ingredients and spices. The chicken is tender and juicy, the chickpeas are creamy and nutty, and the vegetables are colorful and crisp. This dish is perfect for a weeknight dinner or a cozy weekend lunch.

Servings: 4
Prepping Time: 15 minutes
Cook Time: 30 minutes
Difficulty: Easy
Total Time: 45 minutes

Ingredients:
- ✓ 4 chicken breasts, cut into bite-sized pieces
- ✓ 2 tablespoons of olive oil
- ✓ Salt and pepper, to taste
- ✓ 2 teaspoons of curry powder
- ✓ 1 teaspoon of smoked paprika
- ✓ 1/4 teaspoon of cumin
- ✓ 1/4 teaspoon of turmeric
- ✓ 1/4 teaspoon of Aleppo pepper flakes (optional)

- ✓ 1 onion, chopped
- ✓ 3 cloves of garlic, minced
- ✓ 2 carrots, peeled and sliced
- ✓ 1 cauliflower, cut into florets
- ✓ 1 can of chickpeas, drained and rinsed
- ✓ 1/4 cup of chicken broth
- ✓ 1/4 cup of coconut milk
- ✓ 2 tablespoons of lemon juice
- ✓ Fresh parsley, chopped, for garnish

Step-by-Step Preparation:
1. Preheat oven to 200°C (180°C fan-forced) and lightly grease a baking sheet.
2. In a small bowl, whisk together the olive oil, salt, pepper, curry powder, smoked paprika, cumin, turmeric, and Aleppo pepper flakes (if using).
3. In a large bowl, toss the chicken with half of the spice mixture and spread it evenly on the prepared baking sheet.
4. In the same bowl, toss the onion, garlic, carrots, cauliflower, and chickpeas with the remaining spice mixture and scatter them around the chicken.
5. Bake for 25 to 30 minutes until the chicken is cooked and the vegetables are tender.
6. bring the chicken broth and coconut milk to a boil in a small saucepan, then reduce the heat and simmer until slightly thickened about 10 minutes.
7. Drizzle the sauce and lemon juice over the chicken and vegetable mixture and sprinkle with parsley.
8. Enjoy with rice, naan bread, or salad.

Nutritional Facts: (Per serving)
- Calories: 489
- Fat: 18 g
- Carbohydrates: 38 g
- Fiber: 11 g
- Protein: 46 g

You can easily adjust the spiciness and creaminess of the dish to your liking. Try it today, and let me know what you think!

Recipe 40: Chicken Breast Cutlets With Tomato Cream Sauce

If you are looking for a quick and easy chicken dinner that is low in fat and protein, you will love this chicken breast cutlets with sun-dried tomato cream sauce recipe. The chicken is tender and juicy, and the sauce is rich and creamy, with a tangy and savory flavor from the sun-dried tomatoes. This dish is perfect for a busy weeknight, as it can be ready in just 25 minutes. Serve it with your favorite pasta, rice, or salad for a satisfying and delicious meal.

Servings: 4
Prepping Time: 10 minutes
Cook Time: 15 minutes
Difficulty: Easy
Total Time: 25 minutes

Ingredients:
- ✓ 4 chicken breast cutlets (about 1 pound)
- ✓ Salt and black pepper, to taste
- ✓ 2 tablespoons of oil from a jar of sun-dried tomatoes
- ✓ 1/4 cup chopped shallots

- ✓ 1/2 cup dry white wine or vermouth
- ✓ 1/2 cup chicken stock
- ✓ 1/4 cup heavy cream
- ✓ 1/4 cup grated Parmesan cheese
- ✓ 1/4 cup chopped sun-dried tomatoes
- ✓ 2 teaspoons fresh thyme leaves
- ✓ 1 teaspoon dried oregano
- ✓ 1/4 cup chopped fresh basil

Step-by-Step Preparation:

1. Season the chicken cutlets with salt and pepper on both sides.
2. Heat the oil from the sun-dried tomatoes in a large skillet over medium-high heat. Cook the chicken in batches for about 3 minutes per side or until golden and cooked through. Transfer to a plate and keep warm.
3. In the same skillet, stirring frequently, cook the shallots and sun-dried tomatoes for about a minute.
4. Add the wine and chicken stock and bring to a boil. Reduce the heat and simmer until slightly thickened about 5 minutes.
5. Stir in the cream, Parmesan, thyme, and oregano. Season with salt and pepper to taste.
6. Return the chicken to the skillet and spoon some sauce over each cutlet. Sprinkle with basil and serve.

Nutritional Facts: (Per serving)

- Calories: 378
- Fat: 19 g
- Saturated Fat: 7 g
- Cholesterol: 116 mg
- Sodium: 329 mg
- Carbohydrates: 9 g
- Fiber: 1 g
- Sugar: 4 g
- Protein: 39 g

This chicken breast cutlets with sun-dried tomato cream sauce recipe is a great way to enjoy a flavorful and satisfying meal without spending too much time in the kitchen. Enjoy this dish with your family or friends, and don't forget to share your feedback with us. We hope you love it as much as we do.

Chapter 06: Fish And Seafood For Your Heart

Recipe 41: Grilled Salmon With Sauce

Grilled salmon is a healthy and delicious dish that can be enjoyed all year round. This recipe features a simple but flavorful sauce made with ginger, soy sauce, garlic, and maple syrup, adding a sweet and spicy touch to the tender and flaky fish. Serve it with rice, salad, or roasted vegetables for a complete and satisfying meal.

Servings: 4
Prepping Time: 10 minutes
Cook Time: 15 minutes
Difficulty: Easy
Total Time: 25 minutes

Ingredients:
- ✓ 4 (6 ounces) salmon fillets, skin on
- ✓ Salt and black pepper, to taste
- ✓ 1/4 cup soy sauce

- ✓ 2 tablespoons maple syrup
- ✓ 2 tablespoons rice vinegar
- ✓ 1 tablespoon sesame oil
- ✓ 2 teaspoons grated ginger
- ✓ 2 cloves garlic, minced
- ✓ 2 green onions, sliced
- ✓ 1 teaspoon sesame seeds, for garnish

Step-by-Step Preparation:
1. Whisk together the soy sauce, maple syrup, rice vinegar, sesame oil, ginger, and garlic in a small bowl. Reserve 1/4 cup of the sauce for later use.
2. Place the salmon fillets in a large ziplock bag or a shallow baking dish. Pour the remaining sauce over the salmon and turn to coat well. Refrigerate for at least 15 minutes or up to 2 hours.
3. Preheat the grill to medium-high heat, and lightly oil the grate. Remove the salmon from the marinade, and discard the excess. Season the salmon with salt and pepper on both sides.
4. Place the salmon on the grill, skin side down, and cook for about 10 minutes, or until the fish flakes easily with a fork. Flip the salmon halfway through and brush with some of the reserved sauce.
5. Transfer the salmon to a platter and drizzle with the remaining sauce. Sprinkle with green onions and sesame seeds, and serve.

Nutritional Facts: (Per serving)
- Calories: 367
- Fat: 18 g
- Saturated Fat: 3 g
- Cholesterol: 94 mg
- Sodium: 857 mg
- Carbohydrates: 13 g
- Fiber: 0 g
- Sugar: 10 g
- Protein: 38 g

This grilled salmon with sauce and salmon fillet glazed-in ginger sauce recipe is a great way to enjoy a light and nutritious meal full of flavor and texture. Enjoy this dish with your family or friends, and don't forget to share your feedback with us. We hope you love it as much as we do.

Recipe 42: Delicious Fillets of Grilled Coalfish

Pollock or coalfish are lean, mild white fish that are easy to cook and versatile to pair with different sauces and sides. This recipe shows you how to make delicious fillets of grilled or oven-baked pollock or coalfish with a simple lemon and herb marinade that enhances the flavor and moisture of the fish.

Servings: 4
Prepping Time: 10 minutes
Cook Time: 15 minutes
Difficulty: Easy
Total Time: 25 minutes

Ingredients:
- ✓ 4 (6 ounces) pollock or coalfish fillets, skinless and boneless
- ✓ Salt and black pepper, to taste
- ✓ 1/4 cup olive oil
- ✓ 2 tablespoons lemon juice
- ✓ 2 teaspoons lemon zest
- ✓ 2 cloves garlic, minced
- ✓ 2 tablespoons chopped fresh parsley
- ✓ 1 teaspoon dried oregano
- ✓ 1/4 teaspoon red pepper flakes, optional

Step-by-Step Preparation:

1. Rinse the fish fillets and pat them dry with paper towels. Season with salt and pepper on both sides.
2. Whisk together the olive oil, lemon juice, lemon zest, garlic, parsley, oregano, and red pepper flakes in a small bowl. Reserve 2 tablespoons of the marinade for later use.
3. Place the fish fillets in a large ziplock bag or a shallow baking dish. Pour the remaining marinade over the fish and turn to coat well. Refrigerate for at least 15 minutes or up to 2 hours.
4. If grilling, preheat the grill to medium-high heat and lightly oil the grate. If baking, preheat the oven to 375°F, and line a baking sheet with parchment paper or spray it with cooking spray.
5. Remove the fish from the marinade, and discard the excess. Place the fish on the grill or the baking sheet, and cook for about 15 minutes, or until the fish flakes easily with a fork. Flip the fish halfway through and brush with some of the reserved marinade.
6. Transfer the fish to a platter, and garnish with more parsley and lemon slices if desired. Serve hot or at room temperature.

Nutritional Facts: (Per serving)

- Calories: 292
- Fat: 16 g
- Saturated Fat: 2 g
- Cholesterol: 90 mg
- Sodium: 156 mg
- Carbohydrates: 2 g
- Fiber: 0 g
- Sugar: 1 g
- Protein: 35 g

This recipe for delicious fillets of grilled or oven-baked pollock or coalfish is a great way to enjoy a healthy and tasty meal that is easy to prepare and cook. Enjoy this dish with your favorite salad, rice, potatoes, or bread, and don't forget to share your feedback with us. We hope you love it as much as we do.

Recipe 43: Spicy Mexican Shrimp Cocktail With Avocado

Spicy Mexican Shrimp Cocktail is a refreshing and flavorful appetizer perfect for a hot summer day. It consists of cooked shrimp, fresh vegetables, and a zesty tomato-based sauce seasoned with lime juice, hot sauce, and cilantro. This recipe is low in fat and high in protein and can be made in advance and chilled until ready to serve.

Servings: 4
Prepping Time: 20 minutes
Cook Time: 5 minutes
Difficulty: Easy
Total Time: 25 minutes

Ingredients:
- ✓ 1 pound large shrimp, peeled and deveined
- ✓ 2 cups vegetable juice, such as V8
- ✓ 1/4 cup ketchup
- ✓ 2 tablespoons lime juice
- ✓ 1 tablespoon Worcestershire sauce
- ✓ 1 teaspoon hot sauce, or to taste
- ✓ Salt and pepper, to taste
- ✓ 2 tomatoes, diced
- ✓ 1/4 cup chopped red onion

- ✓ 1/4 cup chopped fresh cilantro
- ✓ 1 avocado, peeled and diced
- ✓ Tortilla chips for serving

Step-by-Step Preparation:

1. Bring a large pot of water to a boil. Add the shrimp and cook for about 5 minutes until pink and firm. Drain and rinse under cold water. Cut the shrimp into bite-sized pieces if desired.
2. Whisk together the vegetable juice, ketchup, lime juice, Worcestershire sauce, hot sauce, salt, and pepper in a large bowl. Add the shrimp, tomatoes, onion, and cilantro and toss to combine. Refrigerate for at least 2 hours to let the flavors meld.
3. Just before serving, gently stir in the avocado. Spoon the shrimp cocktail into individual glasses or bowls and serve with tortilla chips.

Nutritional Facts: (Per serving)

- Calories: 269
- Fat: 10 g
- Saturated Fat: 1 g
- Cholesterol: 221 mg
- Sodium: 763 mg
- Carbohydrates: 21 g
- Fiber: 6 g
- Sugar: 12 g
- Protein: 25 g

This spicy Mexican shrimp cocktail recipe is a great way to enjoy a light and delicious appetizer full of fresh and vibrant flavors. Enjoy this dish with your family or friends, and don't forget to share your feedback with us. We hope you love it as much as we do.

Recipe 44: Baked Dijon Mustard Salmon

Enjoy a delicious and healthy meal of baked Dijon mustard salmon wit fingerling potatoes. This dish is easy to make, low in fat, and high in protein It's perfect for a weeknight dinner or a special occasion.

Servings: 4
Prepping Time: 15 minutes
Cook Time: 25 minutes
Difficulty: Easy
Total Time: 40 minutes

Ingredients:
- ✓ 4 (6-ounce) salmon fillets
- ✓ 1/4 cup chopped fresh parsley
- ✓ 3 tablespoons Dijon mustard
- ✓ 2 tablespoons lemon juice
- ✓ 2 tablespoons avocado oil or olive oil
- ✓ 4 garlic cloves, minced
- ✓ Salt and pepper, to taste
- ✓ 1 1/2 pounds fingerling potatoes, halved
- ✓ Fresh parsley for garnish

Step-by-Step Preparation:
1. Preheat oven to 375°F and line a baking sheet with aluminum foil.
2. Whisk together parsley, dijon mustard, lemon juice, oil, garlic, salt, and pepper in a small bowl.
3. Place the potatoes on the prepared baking sheet, drizzle with dijon mixture, and toss to coat. Arrange them in a single layer and bake for 15 minutes or until partially cooked.
4. Remove the baking sheet from the oven and make space for the salmon fillets. Place the salmon skin on the baking sheet and spoon the remaining dijon mixture over the top.
5. Return the baking sheet to the oven and bake for another 10 minutes until the salmon is cooked and the potatoes are tender.
6. Sprinkle some fresh parsley over the dish and serve hot or at room temperature.

Nutritional Facts: (Per serving)
- Calories: 519
- Fat: 23 g
- Carbohydrates: 36 g
- Fiber: 5 g
- Protein: 42 g

This baked dijon mustard salmon with fingerling potatoes is a simple and satisfying meal you can whip up in no time. It's full of flavor, nutrients, and omega-3 fatty acids. You can serve it with a green salad or your favorite vegetable side dish. Enjoy!

Recipe 45: Delicious Mexican Tacos Fish

Tacos arrachera are a classic street food in Mexico, where tender and juicy skirt steak is marinated in a flavorful blend of spices, lime juice, and beer. The steak is then grilled over high heat and chopped into bite-sized pieces. Serve the tacos with warm tortillas, corn pico de gallo, cotija cheese, and jalapeño-avocado aioli for a satisfying and delicious meal.

Servings: 4
Prepping Time: 15 minutes
Cook Time: 15 minutes
Difficulty: Easy
Total Time: 30 minutes

Ingredients:
- ✓ 1 pound skirt steak, cut into 12-inch pieces
- ✓ 1/4 cup lime juice
- ✓ 2 packets season with coriander and annatto
- ✓ 1 tablespoon adobo seasoning
- ✓ 1/4 cup chopped onion
- ✓ 1/2 cup Mexican beer
- ✓ 12 corn or flour tortillas
- ✓ 1 cup corn pico de gallo

- ✓ 1/4 cup crumbled cotija cheese
- ✓ 1/4 cup jalapeño-avocado aioli

Step-by-Step Preparation:
1. Whisk together lime juice, season, adobo, onion, and beer in a shallow dish. Add the steak and turn to coat. Cover and refrigerate for at least 1 hour or up to 24 hours.
2. Preheat a grill to medium-high. Remove the steak from the marinade and discard the marinade. Grill the steak for 6 to 7 minutes per side or until charred and medium-rare. Transfer to a cutting board and let rest for 5 minutes. Cut into small pieces across the grain.
3. Warm the tortillas on the grill or in the microwave. Assemble the tacos by adding some steak, pico de gallo, cheese, and aioli to each tortilla. Fold and enjoy.

Nutritional Facts: (Per serving)
- Calories: 548
- Fat: 23 g
- Carbohydrates: 51 g
- Fiber: 7 g
- Protein: 34 g

This tacos arrachera recipe is a simple and tasty way to enjoy skirt steak, a meat full of flavor and texture. You can adjust the seasonings and toppings to your liking or try different sauces and salsas. This dish is low in fat and protein, making it an excellent choice for a healthy and satisfying meal.

Recipe 46: Mediterranean Trout Fillet With Broccoli

Indulge in the delicate flavors of this low-fat, high-protein dish featuring fried river trout fillet, beautifully garnished with fresh vegetables and a savory mushroom sauce.

Servings: 4 people
Prepping Time: 20 minutes
Cook Time: 30 minutes
Difficulty: Medium
Total Time: 50 minutes

Ingredients:
- ✓ 4 river trout fillets
- ✓ 1 bunch of broccoli
- ✓ 1 bunch of asparagus sprouts
- ✓ 4 potatoes
- ✓ 200g of mushrooms
- ✓ Salt, pepper, and olive oil for seasoning

Step-by-Step Preparation:
1. Season the trout fillets and fry until golden brown.
2. Steam the broccoli and asparagus sprouts.
3. Bake the potatoes until tender.
4. Sauté the mushrooms and blend to make the sauce.
5. Plate the trout, garnish with the vegetables, and drizzle the mushroom sauce on top.

Nutritional Facts: (Per serving)
- Calories: 350 kcal
- Protein: 40g
- Fat: 10g
- Carbohydrates: 30g

Savor the perfect balance of hearty protein and fresh vegetables in this dish. The mushroom sauce adds a touch of gourmet flair, making it a delightful meal for any occasion.

Recipe 47: Fresh Backed Tilapia Fillet

Experience the light, refreshing flavors of this low-fat, high-protein dish. Freshly baked tilapia fillet, seasoned with tangy lemon and aromatic herbs offers a healthy and delicious meal that's as easy to prepare as it is satisfying.

Servings: 4 people
Prepping Time: 15 minutes
Cook Time: 20 minutes
Difficulty: Easy
Total Time: 35 minutes

Ingredients:
- ✓ 4 tilapia fillets
- ✓ 2 lemons
- ✓ Fresh herbs (parsley, dill, thyme)
- ✓ Salt and pepper to taste
- ✓ Olive oil for drizzling

Step-by-Step Preparation:
1. Preheat the oven and season the tilapia fillets with salt, pepper, and herbs.

2. Drizzle with olive oil and top with lemon slices.
3. Bake until the fish is flaky and fully cooked.

Nutritional Facts: (Per serving)
- Calories: 200 kcal
- Protein: 35g
- Fat: 5g
- Carbohydrates: 0g

This baked tilapia fillet with lemon and herbs shows that healthy food can be flavorful and satisfying. It's a perfect dish for those seeking a nutritious, protein-packed meal that doesn't compromise on taste.

Recipe 48: Grilled Scallops With Fruit Salad

Dive into a refreshing, low-fat, high-protein dish that combines the succulence of grilled scallops with the freshness of a fruit salad, all topped with a tangy lemon honey dressing. This recipe is perfect for a light lunch or a dinner starter.

Servings: 4 people
Prepping Time: 20 minutes
Cook Time: 10 minutes
Difficulty: Easy
Total Time: 30 minutes

Ingredients:
- ✓ 12 large scallops
- ✓ 2 cups mixed fruit (strawberries, blueberries, kiwi)
- ✓ Juice of 1 lemon
- ✓ 2 tablespoons honey
- ✓ Salt and pepper to taste

Step-by-Step Preparation:
1. Preheat the grill to medium heat.
2. Season scallops with salt and pepper, then grill for 2-3 minutes on each side.
3. Mix fruit in a bowl.
4. Whisk together lemon juice and honey, and drizzle over the fruit.
5. Top fruit salad with grilled scallops.

Nutritional Facts: (Per serving)
- Calories: 200
- Protein: 25g
- Fat: 2g
- Carbohydrates: 25g

Enjoy this delightful combination of savory scallops and sweet fruit salad, a perfect balance of flavors that will satisfy you yet crave more. It's a testament that healthy eating doesn't have to be boring or bland.

Recipe 49: Fried Catfish With Cornbread Dipped

Indulge in the southern charm of "Fried Catfish with Cornbread dipped in Buttermilk." This low-fat, high-protein dish is a delightful blend of crispy catfish and moist cornbread, offering a unique culinary experience.

Servings: 4 people
Prepping Time: 15 minutes
Cook Time: 30 minutes
Difficulty: Easy
Total Time: 45 minutes

Ingredients:
- ✓ 4 catfish fillets
- ✓ 1 cup cornmeal
- ✓ 1 cup buttermilk
- ✓ 1 cup cornbread mix
- ✓ Salt and pepper to taste
- ✓ Vegetable oil for frying

tep-by-Step Preparation:
1. Dip catfish fillets in buttermilk, then coat with cornmeal.
2. Heat oil in a pan and fry the catfish until golden brown.
3. Prepare cornbread as per the mix instructions.
4. Serve the fried catfish with a side of cornbread.

Nutritional Facts: (Per serving)
- Protein: 28g
- Fat: 10g
- Carbohydrates: 20g
- Calories: 300

avor the fried catfish's richness, the cornbread's sweetness, and the uttermilk's tanginess. This dish is not just a meal but a celebration of flavors nd textures, making your dining experience truly unforgettable.

Recipe 50: Delicious Grilled Swordfish Steaks

Here's a recipe for **Homemade Grilled Swordfish Steaks with Oliv** **Topping** that serves **4 people**. This dish is a **low-fat, high-protein** fish an seafood recipe perfect for a healthy meal. The total time required to prepar and cook this dish is **45 minutes**.

Ingredients:
- ✓ 4 swordfish steaks
- ✓ 1/4 cup olive oil
- ✓ 1/4 cup chopped fresh parsley
- ✓ 1/4 cup chopped fresh basil
- ✓ 1/4 cup chopped fresh oregano
- ✓ 1/4 cup chopped Kalamata olives
- ✓ 1/4 cup chopped green olives
- ✓ 1/4 cup chopped red onion
- ✓ 1/4 cup chopped sun-dried tomatoes
- ✓ Salt and pepper to taste

Step-by-Step Preparation:
1. Preheat the grill to medium-high heat.
2. Mix the olive oil, parsley, basil, oregano, Kalamata olives, green olives, red onion, and sun-dried tomatoes in a small bowl.
3. Season the swordfish steaks with salt and pepper.
4. Brush the swordfish steaks with the olive oil mixture.
5. Grill the swordfish steaks for 4-5 minutes per side or until they are cooked through.
6. Serve the grilled swordfish steaks with the remaining olive oil mixture.

Nutritional Facts (Per serving):
- Calories: 400
- Total Fat: 20g
- Saturated Fat: 3g
- Cholesterol: 100mg
- Sodium: 400mg
- Total Carbohydrates: 5g
- Dietary Fiber: 1g
- Sugars: 2g
- Protein: 45g

This recipe is excellent for swordfish steaks with a delicious olive topping. It's a healthy and flavorful dish that will impress your guests. Enjoy!

Chapter 07: Delight of Vegetarian and Vegan

Recipe 51: Italian Lasagna With Tomato Sauce

I can help you write a recipe for Italian lasagna with tomato sauce, and cheese served with tomatoes. This low-fat, high-protein, vegetarian, and vegan dish serves 4 people. Here is the recipe:

Servings: 4
Prepping Time: 15 minutes
Cook Time: 40 minutes
Difficulty: Easy
Total Time: 55 minutes

Ingredients:
- ✓ 9 lasagna noodles
- ✓ 1 tablespoon of olive oil
- ✓ 1 onion, chopped

- ✓ 3 cloves of garlic, minced
- ✓ 1 (14-ounce) package of firm tofu, drained and crumbled
- ✓ 2 teaspoons of dried basil
- ✓ 2 teaspoons of dried oregano
- ✓ Salt and pepper, to taste
- ✓ 1 (25-ounce) jar of tomato sauce
- ✓ 2 cups of shredded vegan mozzarella cheese
- ✓ 4 medium tomatoes, sliced

Step-by-Step Preparation:

1. Preheat oven to 375°F and lightly grease a 9x13 inch baking dish.
2. Cook the lasagna noodles in a large pot of boiling water for 8 to 10 minutes or until al dente. Drain and rinse with cold water.
3. Heat the olive oil in a large skillet over medium-high heat and sauté the onion and garlic for about 5 minutes, or until soft.
4. Add the tofu, basil, oregano, salt, and pepper and cook for another 10 minutes, stirring occasionally.
5. Spread 1/3 of the tomato sauce evenly over the bottom of the prepared baking dish.
6. Arrange 3 lasagna noodles over the sauce, then spread half of the tofu mixture over the noodles.
7. Sprinkle 1/3 of the vegan cheese over the tofu layer, then top with half the tomato slices.
8. Repeat with another layer of sauce, noodles, tofu, cheese and tomatoes.
9. Finish with the remaining sauce, noodles, and cheese.
10. Bake for 25 to 30 minutes or until the cheese is melted and bubbly.
11. Let the lasagna rest for 10 minutes before cutting and serving.

Nutritional Facts: (Per serving)

- Calories: 467
- Fat: 18 g
- Carbohydrates: 54 g
- Fiber: 7 g
- Protein: 25 g
- Calcium: 320 mg
- Iron: 5 mg

I hope you enjoy this delicious and nutritious vegan lasagna recipe. It is a great way to satisfy your cravings for cheese and pasta without compromising your health. You can serve it with a green salad or garlic bread for a complete meal. Bon appetit!

Recipe 52: Vegan Sushi Rolls With Fresh Vegetables

I can help you write a recipe for vegan sushi rolls with fresh vegetables and quinoa. This is a tasty vegetarian meal that is low in fat and protein. It serves 4 people and is easy to make. Here is the recipe:

Servings: 4
Prepping Time: 15 minutes
Cook Time: 15 minutes
Difficulty: Easy
Total Time: 30 minutes

Ingredients:
- ✓ 1 cup of quinoa, rinsed and drained
- ✓ 2 cups of water
- ✓ 1/4 cup of rice vinegar
- ✓ 2 tablespoons of sugar
- ✓ 1/2 teaspoon of salt
- ✓ 4 nori sheets
- ✓ 1/2 cucumber, peeled and cut into thin strips
- ✓ 1 carrot, peeled and cut into thin strips

- ✓ 1 avocado, peeled and sliced
- ✓ 1/4 cup of vegan cream cheese (optional)

Step-by-Step Preparation:
1. In a small pot, bring the quinoa and water to a boil. Reduce the heat and simmer, covered, for 15 minutes or until the quinoa is fluffy and the water is absorbed.
2. Whisk the rice vinegar, sugar, and salt in a small bowl. Transfer the quinoa to a large bowl and toss with the vinegar mixture. Let it cool slightly.
3. Place a nori sheet on a bamboo mat and evenly spread 1/4 of the quinoa over it, leaving a 1-inch border at the top. Arrange 1/4 of the cucumber, carrot, avocado, and cream cheese (if using) over the quinoa near the bottom edge of the nori sheet.
4. Roll up the nori sheet from the bottom, tucking in the filling as you go, and moisten the top border with water to seal the roll. Repeat with the remaining ingredients to make 4 rolls.
5. Cut each roll into 6 pieces and serve with soy sauce, wasabi, and pickled ginger.

Nutritional Facts: (Per serving)
- Calories: 367
- Fat: 12 g
- Carbohydrates: 58 g
- Fiber: 9 g
- Protein: 11 g

hope you enjoy this delicious and nutritious vegan sushi recipe. It is a great way to enjoy the flavors of sushi without any fish or seafood. You can also customize the fillings with your favorite vegetables or tofu. Have fun and happy rolling!

Recipe 53: Healthy Red Lentils Dahl

I can help you write a red lentil dahl bowl recipe with lime and fresh coriander. This low-fat, high-protein, vegetarian, and vegan dish serves 4 people and is easy to make. Here is the recipe:

Servings: 4
Prepping Time: 10 minutes
Cook Time: 20 minutes
Difficulty: Easy
Total Time: 30 minutes

Ingredients:
- ✓ 1 tablespoon of vegetable oil
- ✓ 1 onion, chopped
- ✓ 2 cloves of garlic, minced
- ✓ 1 teaspoon of cumin seeds
- ✓ 1 teaspoon of turmeric
- ✓ 1 teaspoon of salt
- ✓ 1/4 teaspoon of cayenne pepper (optional)
- ✓ 4 cups of vegetable broth
- ✓ 1 cup of red lentils, rinsed and drained
- ✓ 2 tablespoons of lime juice

- ✓ 1/4 cup of chopped fresh coriander
- ✓ Lime wedges for serving

Step-by-Step Preparation:

1. In a large pot over medium-high heat, heat the oil and sauté the onion and garlic for about 15 minutes, stirring occasionally, until soft and golden.
2. Add the cumin seeds, turmeric, salt, and cayenne pepper (if using) and cook for another minute, stirring constantly, until fragrant.
3. Stir in the vegetable broth and bring to a boil. Add the lentils and reduce the heat to low. Simmer, uncovered, for about 15 minutes, or until the lentils are tender and the liquid slightly thickens.
4. Stir in the lime juice and coriander. Taste and adjust the seasoning if needed.
5. Serve hot, with lime wedges on the side.

Nutritional Facts: (Per serving)

- Calories: 278
- Fat: 5 g
- Carbohydrates: 42 g
- Fiber: 18 g
- Protein: 16 g
- Iron: 6 mg

I hope you enjoy this delicious and nutritious red lentil dahl bowl with lime and fresh coriander. It is a great way to get protein and fiber from plant sources. You can also customize the spiciness level to your liking. Enjoy!

Recipe 54: Delicious Philly Cheesesteak Sandwich With Onions

I can help you write a recipe for a homemade Philly cheesesteak sandwich with onions and peppers. This low-fat, high-protein, vegetarian, and vegan dish serves 4 people and is easy to make. Here is the recipe:

Servings: 4
Prepping Time: 10 minutes
Cook Time: 15 minutes
Difficulty: Easy
Total Time: 25 minutes

Ingredients:
- ✓ 4 hoagie rolls, split and toasted
- ✓ 2 tablespoons of vegan butter
- ✓ 1/4 teaspoon of garlic powder
- ✓ 8 ounces of vegan steak strips, such as Gardein or Upton's Naturals
- ✓ Salt and pepper, to taste
- ✓ 1 tablespoon of vegetable oil
- ✓ 1 large onion, thinly sliced
- ✓ 2 green bell peppers, thinly sliced

✓ 8 slices of vegan provolone cheese, such as Follow Your Heart or Violife

Step-by-Step Preparation:
1. Preheat oven to 375°F and line a baking sheet with parchment paper. Microwave the vegan butter and garlic powder in a small bowl for 15 seconds or until melted. Brush the butter mixture over the cut sides of the hoagie rolls and place them on the prepared baking sheet. Bake for 5 minutes or until lightly toasted.
2. Over medium-high heat, cook the vegan steak strips in a large skillet for about 10 minutes, turning occasionally, until browned and crisp. Season with salt and pepper to taste and transfer to a plate. Keep warm.
3. Heat the oil in the same skillet over medium-high heat and sauté the onion and bell peppers for about 15 minutes, stirring occasionally, until soft and caramelized. Season with salt and pepper to taste.
4. To assemble the sandwiches, divide the vegan steak strips evenly among the bottom halves of the hoagie rolls. Top with the onion and pepper mixture and two vegan cheese slices per sandwich. Cover with the top halves of the hoagie rolls and wrap each sandwich in aluminum foil. Bake for 10 minutes or until the cheese is melted and gooey.
5. Enjoy your homemade Philly cheesesteak sandwiches with some fries or salad while hot.

Nutritional Facts: (Per serving)
- Calories: 489
- Fat: 21 g
- Carbohydrates: 51 g
- Fiber: 6 g
- Protein: 24 g

I hope you enjoy this delicious and nutritious vegan Philly cheesesteak recipe. It is a great way to recreate the classic sandwich with plant-based ingredients. You can customize the sandwich with your favorite vegan cheese or meat alternatives. Have fun and happy cooking!

Recipe 55: Spicy Chickpea and Spinach Curry

This spicy chickpea and spinach curry is a hearty and flavorful dish that is easy to make in one pot. It's low in fat and protein and suitable for vegetarians and vegans. Enjoy it with rice or bread for a satisfying meal.

Servings: 4
Prepping Time: 10 minutes
Cook Time: 20 minutes
Difficulty: Easy
Total Time: 30 minutes

Ingredients:
- ✓ 1 tablespoon of oil
- ✓ 1 onion, chopped
- ✓ 4 cloves of garlic, minced
- ✓ 2 teaspoons of curry powder
- ✓ 1 teaspoon of cumin
- ✓ 1 teaspoon of paprika
- ✓ 1/4 teaspoon of turmeric
- ✓ 1/4 teaspoon of cayenne pepper (optional)
- ✓ Salt and black pepper, to taste
- ✓ 1 (15-ounce) can of chickpeas, drained and rinsed

- ✓ 1 (14.5-ounce) can of diced tomatoes
- ✓ 2 cups of vegetable broth
- ✓ 4 cups of fresh spinach, chopped
- ✓ 1/4 cup of fresh cilantro, chopped (optional)

Step-by-Step Preparation:

. Heat the oil in a large skillet over medium-high heat. Add the onion and garlic and cook for about 15 minutes, stirring occasionally, until soft and golden.

. Add the curry powder, cumin, paprika, turmeric, cayenne pepper (if using), salt, and black pepper and cook for another minute, stirring well to coat the onion and garlic.

. Add the chickpeas, tomatoes, and broth and bring the mixture to a boil. Reduce the heat and simmer for 15 minutes, until the sauce is slightly thickened.

. Stir in the spinach and cilantro (if using) and cook for another 5 minutes, until the spinach is wilted.

. Serve hot with rice or bread, or store in an airtight container in the refrigerator for up to 3 days or in the freezer for up to 3 months.

Nutritional Facts: (Per serving)
- Calories: 282
- Fat: 7.8 g
- Carbohydrates: 42.6 g
- Fiber: 11.3 g
- Protein: 12.4 g

This recipe is inspired by some of the web search results I found for "Spicy Chickpea and Spinach Curry. I hope you like it, and let me know how it turns out.

Recipe 56: Healthy Vegan Mushroom

This healthy vegan mushroom stew is" a cozy and satisfying dish you ca[n] make in"a cast iron skillet. It's low in fat, high in protein, and full [o]f vegetables and herbs. Serve it with some crusty bread or over-mashed It's f[or] a delicious meal.

Servings: 4
Prepping Time: 15 minutes
Cook Time: 25 minutes
Difficulty: Easy
Total Time: 40 minutes

Ingredients:
- ✓ 2 tablespoons of oil
- ✓ 1 onion, diced
- ✓ 4 cloves of garlic, minced
- ✓ 1 teaspoon of dried thyme
- ✓ 1 teaspoon of dried rosemary
- ✓ Salt and black pepper, to taste
- ✓ 8 ounces of baby bella mushrooms, sliced
- ✓ 2 medium carrots, peeled and chopped
- ✓ 2 tablespoons of all-purpose flour

- ✓ 2 cups of vegetable broth
- ✓ 2 tablespoons of soy sauce
- ✓ 2 teaspoons of browning sauce (such as Gravy Master or Marmite)
- ✓ 2 cups of kale, stemmed and chopped
- ✓ 2 tablespoons of fresh parsley, chopped

Step-by-Step Preparation:

1. Heat the oil in a large cast iron skillet over medium-high heat. Add the onion, garlic, thyme, rosemary, salt, and pepper and cook for about 10 minutes, stirring occasionally, until the onion is soft and golden.

2. Add the mushrooms and carrots and cook for another 10 minutes, stirring occasionally, until the mushrooms are browned and the carrots are tender.

3. Sprinkle the flour over the mushroom mixture and stir well to coat. Gradually whisk in the broth, soy sauce, and browning sauce and bring the mixture to a boil. Reduce the heat and simmer for about 5 minutes, stirring occasionally, until the sauce is thickened.

4. Stir in the kale and parsley and cook for another 5 minutes, until the kale is wilted.

5. Enjoy your healthy vegan mushroom stew with some crusty bread or over-mashed potatoes, or store in an airtight container in the refrigerator for up to 4 days or in the freezer for up to 3 months.

Nutritional Facts: (Per serving)

- Calories: 213
- Fat: 9.4 g
- Carbohydrates: 26.9 g
- Fiber: 4.6 g
- Protein: 8.6 g

This recipe is inspired by web search results for "Healthy vegan mushroom stew in a cast iron skillet. I hope you like it, and let me know how it turns out.

Recipe 57: Vegan Black Bean Burgers

These vegan black bean burgers are moist, flavorful, and packed with plant-based protein. They are easy to make with simple ingredients and fresh parsley. Enjoy them on a bun with your favorite toppings or as a cutlet with a salad.

Servings: 4
Prepping Time: 15 minutes
Cook Time: 15 minutes
Difficulty: Easy
Total Time: 30 minutes

Ingredients:
- ✓ 2 (15-ounce) cans of black beans, drained and rinsed
- ✓ 1/4 cup of chopped red onion
- ✓ 1/4 cup of chopped fresh parsley
- ✓ 2 cloves of garlic, minced
- ✓ 2 teaspoons of ground cumin
- ✓ 1 teaspoon of salt
- ✓ 1/4 teaspoon of black pepper
- ✓ 1/4 cup of oat flour (or all-purpose flour)
- ✓ 2 tablespoons of oil for frying

Step-by-Step Preparation:
1. In a large bowl, mash the black beans with a fork or a potato masher until almost smooth, leaving some chunks for texture.
2. Add the onion, parsley, garlic, cumin, salt, pepper, and oat flour and mix well to combine. The mixture should be thick and hold together. If it is too wet, add more flour as needed.
3. Divide the mixture into four equal portions and shape them into patties. You can also use a round cookie cutter or a glass to make them more uniform.
4. Heat the oil in a large skillet over medium-high heat. Cook the patties for about 7 minutes per side until golden and crisp on both sides.
5. Serve the vegan black bean burgers on buns with your favorite toppings, such as lettuce, tomato, avocado, vegan cheese, vegan mayo, ketchup, mustard, etc. Or serve them as cutlets with a salad or a side dish.

Nutritional Facts: (Per serving)
- Calories: 328
- Fat: 10.6 g
- Carbohydrates: 45.8 g
- Fiber: 15.4 g
- Protein: 15.9 g

This recipe is inspired by web search results for Vegan black bean burgers (cutlets) with parsley. I hope you like it, and let me know how it turns out.

Recipe 58: Healthy Vegan Bun Cha Salad

This vegan bun cha salad bowl is a refreshing and satisfying dish with sticky tofu, rice noodles, and crunchy vegetables. It's low in fat, high in protein, and easy to make in 30 minutes. The tangy dressing adds a burst of flavor to this Vietnamese-inspired meal.

Servings: 4
Prepping Time: 15 minutes
Cook Time: 15 minutes
Difficulty: Easy
Total Time: 30 minutes

Ingredients:
- ✓ 8 ounces of rice noodles (vermicelli-style)
- ✓ 1/4 cup of soy sauce
- ✓ 2 tablespoons of maple syrup
- ✓ 1 tablespoon of sriracha sauce
- ✓ 1 teaspoon of cornstarch
- ✓ 14 ounces of extra-firm tofu, drained, pressed, and cut into cubes
- ✓ 2 tablespoons of oil, divided
- ✓ 2 cups of shredded carrots
- ✓ 2 cups of thinly sliced red cabbage

- ✓ 1/4 cup of rice vinegar
- ✓ 2 tablespoons of lime juice
- ✓ 2 tablespoons of mushroom soy sauce (or regular soy sauce)
- ✓ 2 teaspoons of sugar
- ✓ 1/4 teaspoon of garlic powder
- ✓ 1/4 teaspoon of ginger powder
- ✓ 4 cups of chopped lettuce
- ✓ 1/4 cup of chopped fresh cilantro
- ✓ 1/4 cup of chopped fresh mint
- ✓ 1/4 cup of chopped roasted peanuts

Step-by-Step Preparation:

. Cook the rice noodles according to the package directions, then drain and rinse with cold water. Set aside.

. whisk together the soy sauce, maple syrup, sriracha sauce, and cornstarch in a small bowl. Add the tofu cubes and toss to coat. Let them marinate for 0 minutes.

. Heat 1 tablespoon of oil in a large skillet over medium-high heat. Add the tofu cubes and cook for about 15 minutes, turning occasionally, until browned and sticky. Transfer to a plate and keep warm.

. heat the remaining oil over medium-high heat in the same skillet. Add the carrots and cabbage and cook for about 10 minutes, stirring occasionally, until crisp-tender.

. whisk the rice vinegar, lime juice, mushroom soy sauce, sugar, garlic powder, and ginger powder in a small bowl. This is the dressing for the salad.

. To serve, divide the lettuce among four large bowls. Top with rice noodles, tofu, carrots, cabbage, cilantro, mint, and peanuts. Drizzle with the dressing and enjoy!

Nutritional Facts: (Per serving)

- Calories: 545
- Fat: 19.8 g
- Carbohydrates: 72.6 g
- Fiber: 7.2 g
- Protein: 22.4 g

hope you like it, and let me know how it turns out.

Recipe 59: Delicious Chicken Shawarma Wrap

If you love the flavor and aroma of shawarma, you will love this easy homemade chicken shawarma wrap recipe. It's a satisfying and healthy meal that can be enjoyed by everyone, even vegetarians and vegans. You can make it ahead and reheat it when you're ready to serve or enjoy it cold as a picnic or lunchbox treat.

Servings: 4 **Prepping** **Time:** 15 minutes **Cook** **Time:** 2 minutes **Difficulty:** Easy **Total Time:** 40 minutes

Ingredients:
- ✓ 1/4 cup plain yogurt (use dairy-free for the vegan option)
- ✓ 2 tablespoons lemon juice
- ✓ 2 cloves garlic, minced
- ✓ 1 teaspoon salt
- ✓ 1/2 teaspoon cumin
- ✓ 1/2 teaspoon paprika
- ✓ 1/4 teaspoon turmeric
- ✓ 1/4 teaspoon cinnamon
- ✓ 1/8 teaspoon cardamom
- ✓ 1/8 teaspoon cayenne pepper (optional)

- ✓ 1 pound boneless, skinless chicken thighs (use tofu or seitan for vegetarian or vegan option)
- ✓ 4 pita breads
- ✓ 1/4 cup hummus (use store-bought or homemade)
- ✓ 1/4 cup tzatziki (use store-bought or vegan yogurt-based sauce)
- ✓ 2 cups shredded lettuce
- ✓ 1 cup chopped tomatoes
- ✓ 1/4 cup sliced red onion
- ✓ 2 tablespoons chopped parsley

Step-by-Step Preparation:

1. Whisk together the yogurt, lemon juice, garlic, salt, and spices in a small bowl. Place the chicken (or tofu or seitan) in a ziplock bag or a shallow dish and pour the marinade over it. Massage the marinade into the meat or plant-based protein and refrigerate for at least an hour or overnight.

2. Preheat the oven to 375°F and line a baking sheet with parchment paper. Arrange the chicken (or tofu or seitan) on the prepared baking sheet and bake for 20 to 25 minutes or until cooked through and golden. Let it rest for 10 minutes, then slice thinly or chop into bite-sized pieces.

3. Warm the pita breads in the oven or microwave to assemble the wraps. Spread some hummus and tzatziki over each pita, then top with lettuce, tomatoes, onion, parsley, and feta cheese (if using). Add some chicken (or tofu or seitan) and fold the pita to enclose the filling. Enjoy hot or cold, with more sauces if desired.

Nutritional Facts: (Per serving)

- Calories: 433
- Fat: 12 g
- Carbohydrates: 48 g
- Fiber: 7 g
- Protein: 34 g
- Sodium: 813 mg
- Sugar: 7 g

This chicken shawarma wrap recipe is a great way to enjoy the authentic taste of shawarma at home with minimal effort and maximum flavor. It's a crowd-pleaser that will make everyone happy and satisfied. Try it today, and let me know what you think!

Recipe 60: Cauliflower Steaks With Herb

Cauliflower steaks are a great way to enjoy a hearty and satisfying meal without meat. They are easy to make and have a delicious smoky flavor from the grill. The herb sauce is a fresh and tangy complement to the spiced cauliflower, adding color and nutrients. This recipe is vegetarian and vegan-friendly, and it can be served with your favorite side dishes or salads.

☐ **Servings:** 4
Prepping Time: 10 minutes
Cook Time: 10 minutes
Difficulty: Easy
Total Time: 20 minutes

Ingredients:
- ✓ 1 large head of cauliflower, cut into 4 thick steaks
- ✓ 2 tablespoons of canola oil or grapeseed oil
- ✓ Salt and pepper, to taste
- ✓ 1 teaspoon of ground cumin
- ✓ 1 teaspoon of ground turmeric
- ✓ 1/4 cup of fresh parsley, finely chopped
- ✓ 2 tablespoons of fresh mint, finely chopped
- ✓ 1 lemon, zested and juiced

- ✓ 2 teaspoons of olive oil
- ✓ 1 clove of garlic, finely minced
- ✓ A pinch of red pepper flakes, optional

Step-by-Step Preparation:
1. Preheat the grill to medium-high heat. Brush both sides of the cauliflower steaks with canola or grapeseed oil and season with salt, pepper, cumin, and turmeric.
2. Grill the cauliflower steaks for about 5 minutes per side or until tender and charred.
3. Whisk together the parsley, mint, lemon zest and juice, olive oil, garlic, and red pepper flakes in a small bowl. Season with salt and pepper to taste.
4. Serve the cauliflower steaks with the herb sauce drizzled over them or on the side for dipping.

Nutritional Facts: (Per serving)
- Calories: 211
- Fat: 15 g
- Carbohydrates: 18 g
- Fiber: 7 g
- Protein: 6 g
- Sodium: 86 mg
- Sugar: 7 g

This cauliflower steaks with herb sauce and spice recipe is a simple and delicious way to enjoy a plant-based meal that is filling and flavorful. It is perfect for any occasion, whether you want to impress your guests or treat yourself to a healthy and satisfying dinner. Depending on your preference, you can customize the recipe by adding more or less spices, herbs, or lemon. Try it today, and let me know what you think!

Recipe 61: Vegan Sweet Shepherd's

Here's a recipe for a **Vegan Shepherd's Pie with Sweet Potato Mash, Chanterelle Mushrooms, and Lentils** that serves 4 people. This dish is low in fat and high in protein. The preparation time is 30 minutes, and the cooking time is 1 hour. The difficulty level is easy. The total time is 1 hour and 30 minutes.

Ingredients:
- ✓ 2 large sweet potatoes, peeled and chopped
- ✓ 1/2 cup vegetable broth
- ✓ 1 tablespoon olive oil
- ✓ 1 onion, chopped
- ✓ 2 garlic cloves, minced
- ✓ 1 cup chanterelle mushrooms, chopped
- ✓ 1 cup green lentils, cooked
- ✓ 1/2 cup peas
- ✓ 1 tablespoon tomato paste
- ✓ 1/2 teaspoon dried thyme
- ✓ 1/2 teaspoon dried rosemary

✓ Salt and pepper to taste

tep-by-Step Preparation:
1. Preheat the oven to 375°F.
2. Boil the sweet potatoes in a pot of salted water until tender, about 20 minutes. Drain and mash with vegetable broth.
3. In a skillet, heat olive oil over medium heat. Add onion and garlic and cook until softened about 5 minutes.
4. Add mushrooms and cook until they release their liquid, about 5 minutes.
5. Add lentils, peas, tomato paste, thyme, rosemary, salt, and pepper. Cook until heated through, about 5 minutes.
6. Transfer the lentil mixture to a baking dish. Spread the sweet potato mash over the top.
7. Bake for 30 minutes or until the top is golden brown.

Nutritional Facts (Per serving):
- Calories: 300
- Fat: 3g
- Carbohydrates: 55g
- Fiber: 15g
- Protein: 15g

This Vegan Shepherd's Pie with Sweet Potato Mash, Chanterelle Mushrooms, and Lentils is a delicious and healthy meal that is perfect for any occasion. Enjoy!

Recipe 62: Fresh Raw Salmon Fillet With Asparagus

Enjoy a delicious and healthy meal with this easy oven-roasted salmon recipe. Tender salmon fillets are baked with asparagus, lemon, potatoes, and garlic in a buttery sauce that adds flavor and richness. This low-fat, high-protein dish is perfect for a weeknight dinner or a special occasion.

Servings: 4
Prepping Time: 15 minutes
Cook Time: 25 minutes
Difficulty: Easy
Total Time: 40 minutes

Ingredients:
- ✓ 4 salmon fillets (about 6 oz each)
- ✓ Salt and black pepper, to taste
- ✓ 4 tablespoons butter, melted
- ✓ 2 tablespoons lemon juice
- ✓ 4 cloves garlic, minced

- ✓ 1 teaspoon dried parsley
- ✓ 1 pound baby potatoes, halved
- ✓ 1 bunch asparagus, trimmed
- ✓ Lemon slices, for garnish

Step-by-Step Preparation:

1. Preheat oven to 400°F (200°C) and lightly grease a baking sheet.
2. Season salmon fillets with salt and pepper and place them on one side of the prepared baking sheet.
3. Whisk together butter, lemon juice, garlic, and parsley in a small bowl. Drizzle half of the butter mixture over the salmon fillets.
4. Toss potatoes with salt, pepper, and 1 tablespoon of the remaining butter mixture. Arrange them on the other side of the baking sheet.
5. Bake for 15 minutes, then remove from oven and add asparagus to the baking sheet. Toss asparagus with salt, pepper, and the remaining butter mixture.
6. Return to the oven and bake for another 10 minutes, or until salmon is cooked and potatoes are fork-tender.
7. Garnish with lemon slices and serve hot or at room temperature.

Nutritional Facts: (Per serving)

- Calories: 567
- Fat: 29 g
- Carbohydrates: 34 g
- Fiber: 5 g
- Protein: 44 g
- Sodium: 287 mg

This oven-roasted salmon recipe is a simple and satisfying way to enjoy a nutritious meal. The salmon is moist and flaky, the asparagus is crisp and tender, and the potatoes are creamy and flavorful. The lemon-garlic butter sauce adds a zesty, buttery touch that complements the dish. Try this recipe today and see how easy and delicious it is.

Recipe 63: Spinach Spicy Chickpea and Curry

Warm your taste buds with this spicy, satisfying chickpea and spinach curry. This vegan dish is loaded with protein, iron, and fiber and is easy to make in one pot. You can adjust the heat level and serve it with rice or naan bread for a complete meal.

Servings: 4
Prepping Time: 10 minutes
Cook Time: 20 minutes
Difficulty: Easy
Total Time: 30 minutes

Ingredients:
- ✓ 2 tablespoons of oil
- ✓ 4 cloves of garlic, minced
- ✓ 2 teaspoons of curry paste (or more, to taste)
- ✓ 1 (13.5 oz) can of coconut milk
- ✓ 2 tablespoons of peanut butter
- ✓ 2 tablespoons of soy sauce
- ✓ 1 tablespoon of brown sugar
- ✓ 2 (15 oz) cans of chickpeas, drained and rinsed
- ✓ 4 cups of baby spinach

- ✓ 1/4 cup of chopped cilantro
- ✓ 1/4 cup of roasted peanuts, chopped
- ✓ 2 tablespoons of lime juice
- ✓ Salt and red pepper flakes, to taste

Step-by-Step Preparation:

1. Heat oil in a large skillet over medium-high heat. Add garlic and curry paste and cook, stirring, for about 2 minutes or until fragrant.
2. Whisk in coconut milk, peanut butter, soy sauce, brown sugar, and boil. Reduce heat and simmer for about 10 minutes, stirring occasionally.
3. Add chickpeas and spinach and cook, stirring, for about 5 minutes, or until spinach is wilted and chickpeas are heated.
4. Stir in cilantro, peanuts, and lime juice. Season with salt and red pepper flakes, if desired.
5. Serve hot over rice or with naan bread, if desired.

Nutritional Facts: (Per serving)

- Calories: 613
- Fat: 37 g
- Carbohydrates: 54 g
- Fiber: 15 g
- Protein: 21 g
- Sodium: 718 mg

This chickpea and spinach curry is a delicious way to enjoy a vegan and gluten-free meal full of flavor and nutrition. It's creamy, spicy, satisfying, and ready in 30 minutes. You can make it and reheat it or freeze it for later. Try this recipe today and enjoy a cozy and comforting curry.

Recipe 64: Stuffed Butternut Squash

Make this stuffed butternut squash recipe for a hearty and healthy vegetarian meal. This low-fat, high-protein dish is perfect for a cozy dinner or a festive occasion.

Servings: 4
Prepping Time: 15 minutes
Cook Time: 45 minutes
Difficulty: Easy
Total Time: 1 hour
Ingredients:
- ✓ 2 medium butternut squash
- ✓ 2 tablespoons of olive oil, divided
- ✓ Salt and black pepper, to taste
- ✓ 1 cup of quinoa, rinsed and drained
- ✓ 2 cups of vegetable broth
- ✓ 1/4 teaspoon of dried thyme
- ✓ 1/4 teaspoon of dried rosemary
- ✓ 2 tablespoons of butter
- ✓ 8 ounces of mushrooms, sliced
- ✓ 4 cloves of garlic, minced
- ✓ 4 cups of chopped kale
- ✓ 1/4 cup of grated Parmesan cheese

✓ 1/4 cup of chopped parsley

Step-by-Step Preparation:

1. Preheat oven to 375°F (190°C) and line a baking sheet with parchment paper. Cut the butternut squash in half and scoop out the seeds. Brush the cut sides with 1 tablespoon of olive oil and season with salt and pepper. Place the squash halves cut-side down on the prepared baking sheet and roast for 35 to 40 minutes or until tender.

2. Bring the quinoa, vegetable broth, thyme, rosemary, and a pinch of salt to a boil in a medium saucepan. Reduce the heat and simmer, covered, for 15 to 20 minutes, or until the quinoa is fluffy and the liquid is absorbed. Fluff with a fork and set aside.

3. Heat the butter and the remaining olive oil over medium-high heat in a large skillet. Add the mushrooms and garlic and cook, stirring occasionally, for 10 to 15 minutes or until browned and soft. Season with salt and pepper to taste.

4. Add the kale and cook, stirring, for 5 to 10 minutes or until wilted and tender. Stir in the Parmesan cheese and parsley and remove from the heat.

5. When the squash is done, carefully flip them over and scoop out some of the flesh, leaving a 1/2-inch border. Chop the scooped-out squash and add it to the quinoa. Stir well to combine.

6. Spoon the quinoa mixture into the squash halves, mounding it slightly. Sprinkle some more Parmesan cheese on top, if desired. Return the stuffed squash to the oven and bake for another 10 to 15 minutes or until heated and golden.

7. Enjoy your stuffed butternut squash with fresh greens, or serve with a green salad or crusty bread.

Nutritional Facts: (Per serving)

- Calories: 487
- Fat: 19 g
- Carbohydrates: 69 g
- Fiber: 12 g
- Protein: 16 g
- Sodium: 462 mg

This stuffed butternut squash recipe is a delicious way to enjoy a filling and nutritious vegetarian meal. Try this recipe today and see how tasty stuffed butternut squash can be.

Recipe 65: Healthy Greek Yogurt

Start your day with this refreshing and nutritious Greek yogurt parfait. Laye
creamy yogurt with crunchy granola and sweet raspberries, and top with
honey and nuts for extra flavor and texture. This low-fat, high-protein dish i
perfect for a quick breakfast or snack.

Prepping Time: 5 minutes
Cook Time: 0 minutes
Difficulty: Easy
Total Time: 5 minutes

Ingredients:
- ✓ 3 cups of plain Greek yogurt
- ✓ 1 teaspoon of vanilla extract (optional)
- ✓ 2 cups of granola
- ✓ 2 cups of fresh raspberries
- ✓ 1/4 cup of honey
- ✓ 1/4 cup of chopped nuts (such as almonds, walnuts, or pistachios)

Step-by-Step Preparation:

1. In a small bowl, stir the yogurt and vanilla extract together.
2. In four glass jars or bowls, divide half of the yogurt evenly. Sprinkle half of the granola over the yogurt.
3. Add half of the raspberries on top of the granola. Drizzle half of the honey over the raspberries.
4. Repeat with the remaining yogurt, granola, raspberries, and love.
5. Sprinkle the nuts over the top of each parfait.
6. Enjoy immediately or refrigerate until ready to serve.

Nutritional Facts: (Per serving)

- Calories: 462
- Fat: 15 g
- Carbohydrates: 64 g
- Fiber: 8 g
- Protein: 22 g
- Sodium: 81 mg

This Greek yogurt parfait is a delicious way to enjoy a healthy and satisfying meal. The yogurt is rich in protein and calcium, the granola is a good source of whole grains, and the raspberries are packed with antioxidants and vitamin C. The honey and nuts add a touch of natural sweetness and crunch. Try this recipe today and see how easy and tasty it is.

Recipe 66: Avocado Chocolate Mousse Pudding

Indulge in this decadent and guilt-free avocado chocolate mousse pudding. This keto vegan dessert is made with only 5 ingredients and takes minutes to prepare. It's rich, creamy, and satisfying, with no added sugar and only 4.5 grams of net carbs per serving.

Servings: 4
Prepping Time: 10 minutes
Cook Time: 0 minutes
Difficulty: Easy
Total Time: 10 minutes

Ingredients:
- ✓ 2 ripe avocados, peeled and pitted
- ✓ 1/4 cup of unsweetened cocoa powder
- ✓ 1/4 cup of powdered erythritol or another keto-friendly sweetener
- ✓ 1/4 cup of coconut cream
- ✓ 1 teaspoon of vanilla extract

Step-by-Step Preparation:
1. Place the avocados in a food processor or blender and process until smooth and creamy.
2. Add the cocoa powder, sweetener, coconut cream, and vanilla extract and process until well combined and no lumps remain.
3. Transfer the mixture to a bowl and refrigerate for at least an hour or until chilled and firm.
4. Enjoy your avocado chocolate mousse pudding as it is or with some whipped coconut cream, fresh berries, or chopped nuts on top.

Nutritional Facts: (Per serving)
- Calories: 290
- Fat: 25 g
- Carbohydrates: 15 g
- Fiber: 10.5 g
- Protein: 4 g
- Sodium: 14 mg

This avocado chocolate mousse pudding is a simple and delicious way to treat yourself to a healthy, low-carb dessert. The avocado adds healthy fats and creaminess, while the cocoa powder provides a rich chocolate flavor. The coconut cream and sweetener make it extra indulgent and satisfying. Try this recipe today and see how easy and tasty it is.

Recipe 67: Healthy Vegan Raw Carrot Cake

Craving for a moist and delicious carrot cake that is vegan, raw, and healthy? Look no further than this easy recipe that only requires 10 ingredients and 30 minutes to make. This low-fat, high-protein cake is topped with a creamy cashew frosting that will melt in your mouth.

Servings: 4
Prepping Time: 10 minutes
Cook Time: 0 minutes
Difficulty: Easy
Total Time: 10 minutes

Ingredients:
- ✓ 2 large carrots, peeled and chopped
- ✓ 1 1/2 cups oat flour or buckwheat flour
- ✓ 1 cup pitted dates
- ✓ 1 cup dried pineapple or more dates
- ✓ 1/2 cup unsweetened shredded coconut
- ✓ 1/2 teaspoon ground cinnamon
- ✓ 2 cups raw cashews, soaked and drained
- ✓ 2 tablespoons fresh lemon juice
- ✓ 2 tablespoons melted virgin coconut oil

✓ 1/3 cup pure maple syrup

Step-by-Step Preparation:
1. To make the cake, process the carrots, oat flour, dates, pineapple, coconut, and cinnamon in a food processor until well combined and sticky.
2. Press the mixture into a 6-inch springform pan and refrigerate until firm.
3. To make the frosting, blend the cashews, lemon juice, coconut oil, and maple syrup in a high-speed blender until smooth and creamy, adding water as needed.
4. Spread the frosting over the cake and refrigerate until set.
5. Cut into slices and enjoy your vegan, raw carrot cake.

Nutritional Facts: (Per serving)
- Calories: 667
- Fat: 32 g
- Carbohydrates: 89 g
- Fiber: 11 g
- Protein: 15 g
- Sodium: 48 mg

This vegan, raw carrot cake is perfect for any occasion. It's moist, sweet, and full of wholesome ingredients. The cashew frosting adds a layer of richness and decadence, making this cake irresistible. You won't believe how easy and tasty it is to make this healthy dessert. Try this recipe today and enjoy a slice of heaven.

Recipe 68: Sweet Vegan Chocolate Cake

Who says you can't have your cake and eat it too? This vegan chocolate cake is moist, fluffy, and rich in chocolate flavor. It's made with wholesom ingredients and no eggs or dairy. This low-fat, high-protein cake is perfect fo any occasion.

Servings: 4
Prepping Time: 15 minutes
Cook Time: 25 minutes
Difficulty: Easy
Total Time: 40 minutes

Ingredients:
- ✓ 1 1/2 cups all-purpose flour
- ✓ 3/4 cup cocoa powder
- ✓ 1 teaspoon baking soda
- ✓ 1/2 teaspoon salt
- ✓ 1 cup sugar or xylitol
- ✓ 1/2 cup unsweetened applesauce
- ✓ 1/3 cup oil or almond butter
- ✓ 1 cup water
- ✓ 2 teaspoons vanilla extract

✓ 1/4 cup vegan chocolate chips (optional)

Step-by-Step Preparation:
1. Preheat oven to 350°F (177°C) and grease an 8-inch square baking pan.
2. Whisk together the flour, cocoa powder, baking soda, and salt in a large bowl.
3. In a medium bowl, stir together the sugar, applesauce, oil, water, and vanilla extract.
4. Add the wet ingredients to the dry ingredients and mix well. Fold in the chocolate chips if using.
5. Pour the batter into the prepared pan and spread it evenly.
6. Bake for 25 to 30 minutes or until a toothpick inserted in the center comes clean.
7. Let the cake cool completely in the pan before cutting into 16 pieces.

Nutritional Facts: (Per serving)
- Calories: 248
- Fat: 10 g
- Carbohydrates: 39 g
- Fiber: 3 g
- Protein: 4 g
- Sodium: 221 mg

This vegan chocolate cake is a delicious way to enjoy a healthy and satisfying dessert. The cake is soft, moist, and full of chocolate goodness. The applesauce adds natural sweetness and moisture, while the oil or almond butter adds healthy fats and richness. Enjoy this cake plain or with some vegan whipped cream or frosting. Try this recipe today and see how easy and tasty it is.

Recipe 69: Slow Cooker Chicken Taco With Corn

This is Bing. I can help you write a recipe for a "Homemade slow cooker. Make these homemade slow-cooker chicken tacos for a flavorful and easy meal. Juicy chicken is cooked with salsa, spices, and corn in the crockpot, then shredded and served in tortillas. This low-fat, high-protein dish is perfect for busy weeknights or casual gatherings.

Servings: 4
Prepping Time: 5 minutes
Cook Time: 4 hours
Difficulty: Easy
Total Time: 4 hours 5 minutes

Ingredients:
- ✓ 4 skinless, boneless chicken breasts
- ✓ 1 cup salsa
- ✓ 1 package taco seasoning or 2 tablespoons homemade taco seasoning
- ✓ 1/2 cup canned corn, drained
- ✓ 12 corn or flour tortillas
- ✓ Optional toppings: shredded lettuce, cheese, tomato, onion, sour cream, guacamole, cilantro, etc.

Step-by-Step Preparation:

1. Place chicken breasts in a 3-qt. Slow cooker. Sprinkle with taco seasoning and pour salsa over them. Add corn and stir to combine.
2. Cook on low for 4 hours or high for 2 hours or until chicken is tender and easy to shred.
3. Remove the chicken from the slow cooker and shred it with two forks. Return to the slow cooker and toss with the sauce and corn.
4. Warm tortillas in a skillet over medium heat or the microwave for a few seconds.
5. Serve shredded chicken in tortillas with your favorite toppings.

Nutritional Facts: (Per serving)

- Calories: 386
- Fat: 7 g
- Carbohydrates: 47 g
- Fiber: 6 g
- Protein: 37 g
- Sodium: 1010 mg

This homemade slow-cooker chicken taco recipe is a simple and delicious way to enjoy a Mexican-inspired meal. The chicken is tender, juicy, and flavorful; the corn adds sweetness and texture. You can customize your tacos with any toppings you like or serve them with a green salad or rice and beans. Try this recipe today and see how easy and tasty it is.

Recipe 70: Healthy Vegan Blueberry Muffins

Enjoy these moist and fluffy vegan blueberry muffins with a hint of lemon. They are easy to make with simple ingredients and are low in fat and protein.

Servings: 12 muffins
Prepping Time: 10 minutes
Cook Time: 20 minutes
Difficulty: Easy
Total Time: 30 minutes

Ingredients:
- ✓ 1 cup of soy milk
- ✓ 1 teaspoon of apple cider vinegar
- ✓ 2 cups of all-purpose flour
- ✓ 2 teaspoons of baking powder
- ✓ 1/4 teaspoon of salt
- ✓ 1/2 cup of granulated sugar
- ✓ 1/4 cup of canola oil
- ✓ 1 teaspoon of vanilla extract
- ✓ Zest of 1 lemon
- ✓ 1 1/2 cups of fresh blueberries

Step-by-Step Preparation:

1. Preheat oven to 180°C (350°F) and line a muffin tin with paper liners.
2. Whisk together the soy milk and apple cider vinegar in a small bowl and set aside for 5 minutes to curdle.
3. Whisk together the flour, baking powder, and salt in a large bowl.
4. Whisk together the sugar, oil, vanilla, and lemon zest in another bowl.
5. Add the wet ingredients to the dry ingredients and stir until just combined. Do not overmix.
6. Gently fold in the blueberries with a spatula.
7. Scoop the batter evenly into the prepared muffin cups, filling them about 3/4 full.
8. Bake for 18 to 22 minutes or until a toothpick inserted in the center comes clean.
9. Let the muffins cool slightly in the pan before transferring them to a wire rack to cool completely.

Nutritional Facts: (Per serving)

- Calories: 188 kcal
- Fat: 6 g
- Carbohydrates: 31 g
- Protein: 4 g
- Fiber: 2 g
- Sugar: 14 g

These vegan blueberry muffins are perfect for breakfast, brunch, or dessert. They are soft, sweet, and bursting with juicy berries. You can store them in an airtight container at room temperature for up to 4 days or freeze them for up to 3 months. Enjoy!

Conclusion

As you reach the end of **"The Best Low Fat High Protein Cookbook,** reflect on the journey you've embarked upon towards a healthier, mot vibrant you.

You've discovered the power of high-protein, low-fat recipes and how the can transform your eating habits without compromising flavor. **Ell Rosemary's** carefully curated collection has guided you through an array o delicious meals, each promising to nourish your body and delight your palate

With every page turned and every recipe tried, you've taken the necessar steps toward achieving your health and fitness goals. The knowledge you'v gained is not just about cooking; it's about making informed choices tha benefit your overall well-being. You now possess the tools to continue thi journey, experiment with flavors, and create your culinary masterpieces.

Don't let this be the end. Use what you've learned to inspire others, to continue exploring the world of low-fat, high-protein cooking, and to maintain the positive changes you've made in your life. Share you experiences, spread the word about the benefits of this lifestyle, and remember that your health is a lifelong commitment.

Printed in Great Britain
by Amazon

43127487R00086